Praise for *Mortuary Confidential*

"Alternately poignant and peculiar, *Mortuary Confidential* is an insightful glimpse into the real lives of undertakers."

—MELISSA MARR, *New York Times* bestselling author of the Wicked Lovely series

"I have always had an insatiable curiosity of anything that smacks of the tawdry. I suppose the 'goings on' around funeral parlors must fall under this category because I could not put this book down. Fascinating."

—LESLIE JORDAN, Emmy Award–winning actor

"Curious, wildly honest stories that need to be told, but just not at the dinner table."

—DANA KOLLMANN, author of *Never Suck a Dead Man's Hand*

"As unpredictable and lively as a bunch of drunks at a New Orleans funeral."

—JOE R. LANSDALE

"Sick, funny, and brilliant! I love this book."

—JONATHAN MABERRY, multiple Bram Stoker Award–winning author of *They Bite*

Mortuary Confidential

UNDERTAKERS SPILL THE DIRT

Kenneth McKenzie

AND

Todd Harra

Citadel Press
KENSINGTON PUBLISHING CORP.
WWW.KENSINGTONBOOKS.COM

CITADEL PRESS BOOKS are published by

Kensington Publishing Corp.
119 West 40th Street
New York, NY 10018

All Kensington titles, imprints, and distributed lines are available at special quantity discounts for bulk purchases for sales promotions, premiums, fund-raising, educational, or institutional use. Special book excerpts or customized printings can also be created to fit specific needs. For details, write or phone the office of the Kensington special sales manager: Kensington Publishing Corp., 119 West 40th Street, New York, NY 10018, attn: Special Sales Department; phone 1-800-221-2647.

First printing: May 2010

10 9 8 7 6 5

Printed in the United States of America

Library of Congress Control Number 2009937076

ISBN-13: 978-0-8065-3179-3
ISBM-10: 0-8065-3179-7

The following stories have been collected from funeral directors and morticians across the United States. They are based on actual events; details and events have been altered and/or fictionalized to protect confidentialities.

The contributors are identified by their interests/hobbies outside the funeral service profession as a way to portray their multi-faceted lives.

Death ... It's the only thing we haven't succeeded in completely vulgarizing.

—ALDOUS HUXLEY

Contents

Introduction

by Todd Harra

My great-great-great-grandfather was a cabinetmaker, known as a tradesman undertaker, in rural Delaware. His son, my great-great-grandfather, was an undertaker, and my uncle is one, too. So I guess you could say that undertaking is our family business. It's not uncommon to find that at many funeral homes across the United States, generations of stewards have cared for the dead. Unlike me, however, with my lineage in the business, my co-author, Ken, chose to make it his career.

Ken became interested in funeral directing after his father committed suicide when he was a young boy. While working through his grief, Ken decided to dedicate his life to serving others who are going through their own time of loss. Ken has been in the business a lot longer than I have, well over twenty years, while I have been in it about five. Ken has lived his whole life on the sun-drenched California coast, while I have lived in the east. Our differing ages and geographic locations lead to slightly differing outlooks on the profession and will, we hope, give you a well-rounded look at the industry as a whole.

First, to answer a question I've often been asked, and I'm sure you're wondering, let's nail down the terms undertaker, funeral director, and mortician. The definition for mortician is somewhat ambiguous but connotes someone who works at a mortuary, in both the business and scientific aspects. If you actually break the word down the exact definition would be: a person who has skill or art with the dead. The words funeral director and undertaker are interchangeable, and I'll use them as such throughout the book. Funeral director is the modern, P.C. description of the job title, while undertaker is an old vestige of a term dating back to the colonial period. Either name you use, an undertaker or funeral director is a professional, licensed by the state he practices in to conduct funerals and manage all the details that accompany a death.

So what does an undertaker do?

To put it simply: we care for the dead. To some it might seem an extraordinary profession, macabre even, but one measure of a society is in how it honors its dead. Obviously, the dead don't care—they're dead after all, right?—so the question remains, why should we? The answer is that we, as a society, must uphold a basic principle of humanity, the sanctity of life, through reverence for the dead. As undertakers we're charged with seeing to it that each person who comes through our door is treated with respect and given a dignified funeral. It's a task that has been honed through thousands of years of history.

The profession of undertaking and embalming is as ancient as the pyramids of Egypt. And we, the keepers of the dead, have been regarded through history by some as honorable, and others as a necessary evil. We have a heavy burden to carry sometimes, but the burden is made worthwhile when the bereaved members of a family are able to bury a loved one properly and move on with their lives.

I participate in a program sponsored by a local university. Called "What's My Line?" the program gets professionals into elementary schools to give kids a look at various careers. Basically, it's "twenty questions;" the kids ask me yes-or-no questions and then try to guess what I do. Only one class has ever guessed correctly. I guess I shouldn't be shocked. A funeral director is a "hidden" professional, only consulted when there is a need. Death isn't convenient in our culture. In fact, it represents a failure to our scientific/medical-oriented society. No wonder kids don't want to be funeral directors when they grow up; they don't even know the profession exists. Sure, undertakers sponsor little league teams, advertise in the local paper, and may support a local channel, but that's typical of the press we get—"purchased" press.

When we do get national press, it always seems to be negative. America is a death-denying, death-defying culture, and the media reflects that. The TV channels and newspapers will run the sensational stories of the one-percentile of bad apples, the shysters. Proper funerals don't make headlines. But it doesn't have to be that way.

When President John F. Kennedy was assassinated, the nation came together and mourned. Everyone remembers that iconic picture of John Kennedy, Jr. saluting his father's passing caisson. That image is the epitome of what a funeral is supposed to accomplish: help people to face a death, acknowledge a life well lived, and express their grief in a public forum. A nation healed together during that funeral of one of America's great leaders.

Our goal in writing this book was to give the readers a look into our world, from *our* perspective, not the salacious media's. TV shows like *Family Plots* and *Six Feet Under* did a lot for the profession by spinning it in a positive way, and we want to bring you more of that type of spin. But instead of from Hollywood, this time it's from the front lines.

Starting with eighty half-baked musings, we distilled them into fifty readable stories that run the gamut of subjects within the profession. To protect the privacy of the contributors, we changed most of the names (except Ken's and mine) and adjusted the settings. In stories that might have contained potentially confidential material, details were altered but the point the contributor was trying to make was retained. Without capitalizing on anyone's loss, we've sought to take a look at the lifestyle of an undertaker, learn a little about the job, and examine some of the thoughts of funeral directors.

The stories range from humorous to poignant. Now, you may ask, "How can *any* aspect of *that* job be humorous?" Read on, and find out. It's not all doom and gloom, and I think you'll enjoy the ride, even though it may be a somewhat darker ride than you're used to. We're going to take you on a step-by-step journey, from "bedside to graveside." There is a lot of mystery and myth surrounding our profession. But a lot of life lessons can be learned from death, as you'll find in the ensuing pages.

We hope these stories will debunk some myths, answer some questions, and give you a glimpse into our daily lives. While no means all-inclusive, or applicable to the entire profession, we think these anecdotes are an interesting, informative cross-section of the job.

Enjoy.

Mortuary Confidential

PART I

First Calls and Removals

When a death happens, the family contacts the neighborhood funeral home. This initial report of the death is known in the profession as the "first call." Soon after it, the remains of the dearly departed are removed from the place of death and brought back to the mortuary for preparation. Unfortunately, the dead have no sense of time; they pass from this life to eternity at all hours of the day and night. And we, the undertakers, are often summoned out of deep sleep, away from the dinner table, and out of the shower, sometimes in bitterly cold weather, to perform the removal.

When we start in this business, we generally exchange an apprenticeship for being on call for the firm. Consequently, the apprentice is usually the one to take the first call and make the removal. The apprentice can sometimes have a difficult job. Depending on the company, the hours can be long and relentless. But as in every other business, you have to start at the bottom. Typically, as you'll see illustrated in several stories throughout the book, apprentices are given an apartment in the funeral home while they serve their tenure.

In the 19th and early 20th centuries, most removals were made from the home. Some of the old-timers I work with can remember some of the old-timers they worked with who would embalm people right in their beds (by a method called gravity injection) and then make the funeral arrangements at the kitchen table with the family, usually with a bottle of spirits in the middle of the table. This was back when people were laid out in the parlors of their homes on cooling boards, and the wakes would be big social events. An old family friend, who isn't an undertaker, likes to tell me about helping one of the local morticians in the '40s, doing removals using wicker baskets instead of the stretchers we now use. Interestingly enough, that is rumored to be where the term "basket case" comes from. Things have changed since then. Bodies are prepared at the funeral home, and most wakes are held at the funeral home or church.

As America shifted from a predominately rural, agrarian society to an urban, industrial/technology-based nation, the sick and dying were shifted from the home to institutional care. Nowadays, most removals are made from hospitals and nursing facilities. Thanks to the emergence of the hospice program, there seems to be a rising number of home deaths. People can once again die at home, in their bed, surrounded by loved ones.

The stories in this section include house calls as well as removals from hospitals/nursing facilities—both of which, as you'll see, can present some...interesting challenges.

CHAPTER 1

The Scream

Contributed by an amateur boxer

I 've been in the business of death many, many years. I've met a lot of different people; seen a lot of deaths, many tragic; and been in too many strange situations to count, much less remember. Today I'm older and grayer, and my memory is fading a little, but there is one incident of a middle-of-the-night body removal that I will never forget as long as I'm not laying on *my* porcelain embalming table.

I can still picture in my mind the house where I heard a dead man scream.

I started out working for my dad's best friend, a man I called my "uncle." He ran a funeral home in a small city with a sprawling suburb. We serviced a fairly large geographic location and a very diverse demographic. On night calls, you never knew what end of the county you'd end up in or what type of people you'd be dealing with.

On the night of this particular event, I happened to be taking the calls with my uncle. In typical fashion, the phone rang in the wee morning hours. I fumbled for the receiver and grunted, "Hello?"

"Death call," my uncle replied. "Meet me up at the funeral home."

I mumbled something unintelligible and hung up. Instead of lying in bed and contemplating another five minutes of darkness, the best thing to do was just hop up—like ripping off the proverbial Band-Aid. I threw on my suit, knotted my tie, donned my topcoat, opened both eyes, and cruised up the highway to the funeral home in my beat-up Buick.

At the office, I loaded the station wagon with the supplies we would need and warmed the engine until my uncle arrived. Once he arrived, we drove a hundred yards to an all-night-diner, as was our routine, fueled up on caffeine, and set out again.

It was just a few days after the New Year, and as we drove through the suburbs, faux candles lit the way from windowsills. The occasional Christmas tree could be seen peeking from a passing house.

"Here it is," my uncle told me, after we turned down a few quiet, tree-lined streets.

"Think so? Not too many cars," I replied.

My uncle consulted his note. "Yep, this is it. Look at the lights." And it was true. Every single light in the house was turned on— a sure sign of a death.

I backed the big old boat of a wagon slowly into the vacant driveway and we got out. The house was a rancher that had fallen in benign neglect; mold grew on the sides of the house and we had to push bare branches out of the way as we navigated the front walkway. My uncle knocked, and I buried my hands deep into my topcoat pockets. It had to be one of the coldest nights of the year.

"Oh, hello," the middle-aged woman who answered the door said. "Thank you for coming this quickly so late."

"That is what we do," my uncle replied.

Introductions were made. Then the woman, Sue, gave my uncle the wounded expression that I had seen scores of times before, and my uncle thousands. It was the look of loss. "Come on in," she said somberly. "Dad is in the back room."

We trooped in, grateful to get out of the biting cold. By habit I stamped my snowless shoes on the mat as I crossed the threshold.

"This is my husband, Harold," Sue said, and gestured to a man standing on the opposite side of the living room. He nodded at us and we both nodded back. "And that is Peaches." Peaches was a large orange tabby sitting on the dining room table near Harold. She watched us with hooded eyes.

"Hi Peaches," my uncle said. Having a cat of his own, he considered himself a cat person. He made a sucking sound with his mouth and Peaches's attitude shifted. The bright ball of fur meowed and ran over to rub against his legs.

"There are more running around here," Sue said.

My uncle smiled. I could tell he liked Sue and Harold because they were cat people.

"Dad's back this way," Sue said and headed towards the rear of the house.

We followed. The rooms were neither tidy nor messy; they were lived-in and had the pleasant aroma of fresh evergreen and holiday candles. Sue and her husband were old enough to have grandchildren, and the remnants of gifts for little children were strewn in our path. The three of us arrived at a bedroom at the back of the house, Harold trailing somewhere behind us. The room appeared to have been a porch at one point and we stepped down into it.

Sue's dad lay on an old cot that looked like an iron camp bed. He was a little lump swaddled in white. Even the small bed dwarfed his tiny size. A small gold crucifix decorated a wall, but, overall, the room looked like a storeroom, which it probably was before Sue's father moved in.

"Oh, Dad," Sue said and she plopped next to him.

As she sat down, a bloodcurdling scream discharged from the bed. The shriek was louder than a drill sergeant's bullhorn. It was a sound straight from hell.

My entire body went rigid and (I swear to this day) blood froze in my veins. Sue jumped up as though she'd been electrocuted and flew across the room to the safety of a corner.

I stole a wide-eyed glance at my uncle. He had seen everything in his years as an undertaker. At that moment, though, he was a shell-shocked soldier. With his mouth agape and eyes wide, he clearly wanted to run. Like me, he stayed put, scared stiff by the scream from a dead man. I am not very religious or superstitious, but standing in that room, I felt a powerful energy course through me.

Harold, behind us in the hallway, was the only one with any composure. He strode in, got down on his knees, and dragged a squalling black cat out from underneath the bed. When he let go of the cat's scruff, it fell over, writhing and still screaming.

"Oh my gosh! Is Ridley alright?" Sue wailed. She rushed over to the cat.

"Your father is dead, tend to him," Harold said briskly. "I'll take care of Ridley." With that, Harold scooped up the squalling cat and took it from the room. My uncle and I made some comments to the effect of "that poor cat," but we were really trying to mask our feelings of terror.

We made the removal without any further surprises, and back in the station wagon, we sat in the driveway with the engine idling for a minute. "I thought—I thought—" I said, but was unable to complete the sentence.

My uncle said nothing but crossed himself.

The next day Sue and Harold stopped by the funeral parlor, with Ridley the cat, to make arrangements for Sue's dad. They had just come from the vet's office, where Ridley's leg had been set in a cast. My uncle insisted they bring the poor thing in rather than have it wait in the cold car. It was both sad and comical to watch the furry survivor, with his look of obvious irritation, hobbling stiff-legged around the parlor while his masters made funeral arrangements.

To this day, whenever I see a black cat, my mind flashes back to that cold night years ago when I heard a dead man scream.

CHAPTER 2

Lost in Translation

Contributed by a food bank volunteer

I was having a dream that I was late for class. The bell kept ringing and ringing, but I couldn't seem to run down the hall fast enough to make it to class in time. That's when I woke up.

Reality was much, much worse. The phone next to my bed was ringing off the hook. I blinked my eyes several times at the bedside clock. It was one of those old alarm clocks where the tumblers turn over new digits. A tumbler turned and the new time read: 4:17.

I cursed and then blanched. My mouth felt like it was filled with cotton and cigarette butts. Next to me, the girl I had met at the party, and whose name I couldn't remember, stirred. The phone trilled again and I snatched it off the hook. "What?" I growled.

It was my boss. It was a death call.

I took down the address, and slammed the phone back into its cradle. I cursed again, this time loudly, and flopped back into my pillow. The city's lights filtered in through my uncurtained windows and played across the ceiling. I tried to focus on the bars of light. It didn't work. Last night's and this morning's party had agreed with me too much. The last time I had glanced at the clock had been only two hours prior, and my lady friend and I were hardly in the throes of passion then. I had probably only been out for an hour.

Idiot! Idiot! I mentally berated myself. I knew better than to drink too much when I was taking death calls, but one vodka and soda begets another and I started having too good a time. I threw off the sheets and summoned the courage to climb out of bed. I stumbled my way across the remnants of party clothing littering the floor. When I flicked on the bedroom lights the inert form beneath the sheets didn't even move.

I did the best job I could dressing myself and on my way out of my loft stopped in the kitchenette and chugged a gallon of water. My place, in the old industrial district of the city, was only a few blocks away from the mortuary, so I didn't have far to go. Walking in the crisp air helped clear my mind.

I got the old station wagon loaded up with a cot and headed for the convalescent hospital. I drove down into the bowels of the hospital and parked by the loading dock. The smell of rotting garbage and soiled sheets in the contained basement assaulted my senses and I staggered to the front of the wagon to empty my guts. When I had collected myself enough to unload the stretcher, I went inside to the nurse's station.

"Hello," I said, trying to smile even though I felt like crap.

I was half-drunk, half-asleep, and the nurse spoke half-English. She glowered at me. "Helwoe," she replied.

I don't want to be up either, lady, I thought, and returned the sour look.

"I'm here for—" I had to think for a moment—"Betty Hancock."

She looked at me with a puzzled expression.

"She's dead," I said in a voice reserved for small children and animals, "and I'm here from the mortuary to get her."

She gave me a blank look.

"Dead!" I gave her a hard stare that finally got her in gear.

She shuffled some papers, made a hushed phone call, and then shuffled some more papers and pointed down the hall. "Forry-sen Bee."

"Forty-seven B?" I repeated.

"Yes," she said, agitated. "Forry-sen Bee!"

I shot her a withering stare and loped down the hall, my head pounding. It felt like I walked down three miles of ammonia-smelling, tiled hell before I arrived at Room 47. Thankfully, the residents were all asleep. I didn't waste time on ceremony and steered the cot into the room. I jockeyed it up next to bed B and went around to the other side of the bed and yanked the sheet down. The person under the sheets moaned, arms flailing in the air.

I let out a scream as I jumped back. I caught my breath and quickly threw the sheet back over the patient. That seemed to soothe her and she (I think it was a she) became still. I rushed out of the room and checked the room number. It was forty-seven. I was about to run down the hallway to scream at the nurse for her incompetence when a light bulb went off in my aching head. I went over to bed D. Sure enough, there was Mrs. Hancock.

As I wheeled her out of the hospital I nodded at the nurse and said, "Forty-seven D—just where you said she'd be." The nurse looked at me like I was crazy.

Later that night, after a long, miserable, hung-over day at the mortuary, I had just laid down in bed to get some much-needed rest when the phone rang. I cursed and grabbed the forever-offending thing. "What?" I yelled, expecting another death call. It was the girl I had left before dawn.

"Whoa, you sound mad," she said.

"Sorry," I said. "I thought it was someone else calling."

"Obviously. Say, what happened to you this morning? I don't even know what time you left. I was kind of confused when I woke up. I thought maybe you had ditched me or something."

"Work," I said and massaged my eyeballs.

"Work?"

"Yeah, and you wouldn't believe the day I had."

"Try me."

I did. Now I'm married to that girl and we have three grown children. My wife's name is Liz, or Elizabeth, which is sometimes Betty.

CHAPTER 3

Patch Out

Contributed by a tennis player

I t was summertime, an early Friday morning, when I got trapped with the talkers. I was looking forward to a nice relaxing weekend at the lake, where I had pitched in with a bunch of friends to rent a cabin for the summer. My girlfriend and I were both "weekend warriors" at the house, and I knew there was a lounge chair on the dock waiting for me that afternoon, so I didn't even mind that much taking a death call at 5 A.M.

When I arrived at the house, I backed the van into the driveway to be as discrete as possible. It was one of those Cracker Jack box houses constructed after the Second World War to accommodate the population explosion. The place looked well maintained and the yard was neat. I guessed the couple had bought the house in the late '40s after the gentleman was discharged from the service and that they had lived there ever since. Sure enough, once I was inside, I found old pictures of the decedent in his military uniform on walls of the bedroom where he lay.

I surveyed the scene, got my equipment, and made the removal.

As I left the house, pushing the gentleman on a cot, the children—a son and two daughters—followed me out; their mother chose to remain inside. For some reason the children felt it was imperative that they make *all* the funeral arrangements right then and there in the front yard at 5:30 in the morning.

I tried to interrupt at numerous points during their rapid dialogue and let them know they would have plenty of time to fulfill their father's funeral wishes when they came in for the arrangement conference later in the day. When that didn't work, I started edging closer to the van with the cot, hoping they'd get the hint. They didn't.

The paperboy drove by gawking at the draped figure on the cot. I tried using his presence as a distraction to wrap things up. It didn't work. One of the daughters merely picked up the paper while trying to talk over the other two.

I stood at the rear of the van for as long as I could bear, but when I realized they were never going to stop, I decided to load their father in front of them, hoping that maybe then they would get the hint.

They didn't get it then either.

They continued talking while I placed their father in the van and slammed the doors. They talked some more while I stood outside and stamped my feet. Even though it was summer, it is cold in the arid climates in the early morning and I had forgotten my jacket.

The paperboy rode back by, this time a lot slower. He wanted more of the show. The daughter with the paper in her hand waved. I wanted to bury my head in my hands.

Finally, I hopped in the van and started the engine and turned on the heater. Still they talked, now over the roar of the idling engine, each one thinking of something and throwing it out, and the others would hop onto that new bandwagon. In mortuary school I had been taught, in painstaking detail, the virtue of patience and politeness. But my patience was gone. After almost 45 minutes in their driveway, I had yet to say a word! Tired of trying to cut in gracefully, I announced it was time for me to leave and said I would call them in a couple of hours, after they had some time to think.

So frazzled was I by the three talkers that I accidentally gunned the engine and dropped it into drive at the same time. The van made a loud screech as the tires spun. I rocketed out of the driveway at a speed a NASCAR driver would have envied. I barely had time to spin the wheel hard to avoid careening into the neighbor's front yard. I looked in the rearview mirror and saw two nice thick sets of burnt rubber on their driveway.

The cardinal rule of leaving after a house call is to drive as slowly as possible. It gives the family a sense of security knowing their loved one is safe and sound, and, unlike me on that day, not in the hands of some madman.

I remember thinking as I drove down their street, a little slower: *I hope they didn't get the wrong impression.*

CHAPTER 4

The Fly Swatter Saga

Contributed by a fitness buff

I t was June. I remember because my partner and his wife always take the last week of June and go on a cruise. That summer they were in the Mediterranean. While they were being waited on hand-and-foot and sipping tropical libations, I was back home trying to keep the shop running.

Of course, with my usual luck, I received a call that someone had died at our local hospital in the early hours of the morning. Normally, a hospital removal isn't a big deal at all; one person can do it, except that I have the nasty habit of nodding off while I'm driving at night. I have a form of sleep apnea, and, although I wear a Darth Vader mask when I sleep, I am still prone to napping while driving. The rumble strips have saved my life more than once, and it's not nearly as funny as when Chevy Chase did it.

Generally my partner, Chuck, will drive us at night or just go by himself, but since there was no Chuck, my wife, Sammy, offered to drive me to the hospital. She stipulated that she'd only do it if she didn't have to dress up or get out of the van. I gratefully accepted her terms.

We made the long forty-five minute trek to the hospital, which at that time of the night was closed for all intents and purposes. I signed the necessary paperwork at the front desk and then directed my wife around the building to the loading dock where the removals are made. I left her listening to the new Rascal Flatts CD in the van and met the sleepy orderly at the back door.

The orderly led me down the familiar path of twisting hallways and anterooms that led toward the morgue and then helped me transfer the remains. I bid him adieu after giving him a little something for his help and saw myself out through the bowels of the hospital.

I banged against the crash bar to the back door and passed through. It closed with a loud *click*. Sammy, seeing me coming down the ramp with the body, hopped out of the van, slammed the door, and went around to open the rear panel doors.

They were locked. She ran around to the passenger side to unlock the rear doors, but it was locked too. So was the driver's door.

Unfortunately, in her zeal to help me she had hit the automatic locking button.

No problem, I told myself, *I'll just call the front desk*. I reached for my cell phone and remembered, *it's in the pocket of my suit, which is…in the van*. So there I stood with my barefoot wife behind a locked, vacant hospital with a locked, idling van in the middle of the night as we contemplated the body on the cot.

"What do we do now?" my wife asked.

I looked at her and raised an eyebrow. I wasn't mad at her. She had only been trying to help, after all. But I paused before I spoke to make sure no angry words would come out. She used the pause to ask, "Is there a phone in there?" She gestured to the door I had just exited from. "Perhaps we could call the cops to come and pop the lock."

I shook my head. "Cops don't do that anymore. Besides, even if there was a phone inside that door, it's locked this time of night."

She shrugged and asked for the second time, "What do we do now?"

Good question.

We talked about calling for a locksmith, but the closest one was in our town, forty-five minutes away, so we nixed that idea. There were spare keys to the van hanging at the funeral home, and we batted around the names of several people we could call at this time of night to bring the keys out to us, but we didn't want to ask anyone such a huge favor. I had never popped a car lock before but decided this was a good time to try. First I needed some tools.

"You want to come with me to the front desk or do you want to stay here?" I asked Sammy.

"What about the body?" she protested.

"I care more about your safety right now. The body will be fine here alone for a few minutes at this time of night."

"I can't let anyone see me like this! I'll stay here," Sammy said. And indeed, besides being barefoot, she was only wearing a tiny pair of sweat shorts and a novelty spaghetti-strap top that was a spoof on the milk commercial. It read: Got Formadehyde? I had given it to her as a joke for Christmas; she of course never wore it outside the house. Sammy is the type of woman who would rather (excuse the pun) die than have anyone see her dressed so inappropriately.

"Suit yourself," I told her and set out to make the long trek around the hospital. It took me what seemed like ages to hike around the sprawling medical complex. *Where are those little trams when you really need them?* I remember grumbling to myself at one point. During the day the hospital has courtesy golf carts to ferry people around. Not so much at the witching hour.

I was sweating bullets by the time I marched through the front door. The receptionist gave me a surprised look when I strode up to her for the second time and asked politely, "Could I please borrow a metal coat hanger?"

She laughed. "Honey, we ain't got nothing like that here."

I explained the situation and the grin on her face got wider. When I finished my saga she said, "Wait here. Let me go see what I can find." She disappeared and after a few minutes re-appeared with an old fashioned fly swatter. "Here. Try this. It's the only thing I could find."

I gingerly took it, thanked her, and made my way back to my van, this time through the hospital. The vehicle still sat idling with the cot resting next to it, but my wife was gone. I looked all around. No Sammy. "Sammy?" I called. "Sammy?"

She came around one of the dumpsters, picking her way delicately through the scattered trash.

"What were you doing?" I asked.

"I didn't want anyone to see me like this! So I found a chair the employees use during their smoke breaks and was just waiting. Did you get it?"

I showed her the fly swatter, its yellow plastic mesh surface speckled with the mangled pieces of its victims. Sammy grimaced. "Sorry, it's all the lady at the front desk could find. Let's keep our fingers crossed."

I bent the white wire handle into a hook and jammed it between the glass and gasket of the window and made a motion like I was churning butter. Nothing happened. I twisted the wire. It got stuck. Sweat rolled off my face, as I gave it more elbow grease. I was about to call it quits when I angled the wire down and felt it catch. I gently pulled toward the side mirror and it slipped. I released a stream of language that made Sammy blush; wiped my face with my shirtsleeve and repeated the same procedure. The second time I felt the lock click.

Victory!

I loaded the body into the rear of the van and we drove back to the front of the hospital. I bent the wire handle of the fly swatter back into its original configuration as best as I could and proudly returned it to the receptionist.

My wallet now contains a spare set of keys.

CHAPTER 5

Business Hours

Contributed by an artistic gymnastics competitor

I t was one of the usual morning staff meetings. All the guys I work with sat guzzling their coffee and I sipped on my Mountain Dew. I can't stand coffee. I can't figure out how they can drink it all day long. In fact, I won't even date guys that drink it. That's how much it grosses me out.

As with most morning meetings, I was bored. Our manager, Hunter, is a numbers guy. So we have to hear about casket sales this quarter compared to this point last quarter. Up. Down. He whines either way. *Just give us our daily assignments and be done with it,* I want to scream. But I don't. I just sit there and sip my green soda and hope Hunter and his spreadsheets will get devoured by a pack of rabid beavers on his way home. I say this because Hunter looks like Howdy Doody, and Howdy Doody is made of wood...you get the picture. I was entertaining my usual beaver fantasy when an old woman poked her head into the employee lounge.

"Can I help you?" Howdy Doody asked. He was clearly annoyed at being interrupted while discussing the things we could do to increase fuel economy in the company fleet.

"Oh, dear. I hope I'm not interrupting," the woman said. She looked like a sweet old grandmother.

"No, you're not," Howdy Doody said in a tone that suggested otherwise.

"My husband died," the old woman said.

"Oh, my. I am sorry," Howdy Doody said. He didn't sound sorry. *Pick me! Pick me!* I silently willed him.

"Heather will help you take care of everything," he said and made a motion with his head as if to dismiss me.

Needing no further urging, I nearly ran out of the meeting. As I turned the corner I heard Howdy Doody pick up his monologue where he left off.

I led the frail old woman, whose name I learned was Mrs. Brewer, to the arrangement conference room and poured her a glass of water to drink while I went and gathered my papers. "Okay, Mrs. Brewer," I said when I returned, "when did your husband die?"

"Last night."

I wrote down the previous day's date on my paper. "Which hospital did he die at?" I assumed it was a hospital because a nursing home surely would have called us to come take his remains as soon as he passed.

"He died at home," she said matter-of-factly.

"Home?"

"Yes, that's what I said."

"Last night?"

"Yes," she sounded slightly annoyed at being questioned, but looked so meek and mild sitting across the vast conference table from me. Her withered hands were folded neatly on the polished surface.

"Mrs. Brewer?"

"Yes, dear?"

"Why didn't you call us to come pick your husband up last night?" I asked slowly, trying not to sound patronizing.

"Oh, dear," she said and waved a hand at me, "it was far too late, nearly half past eight. You wouldn't have been open; it was too late."

"We never close—" I stopped and collected my thoughts. "You can always call us. Anytime. Day or night. We're a funeral home. That's what we do."

"Well, it was no matter, Heather, dear. I got to sleep next to him one last time. The only thing was that I had to vacuum the ants off of him this morning. I didn't want them on him when you all arrived." She smiled at me.

I shivered.

"Okay, well," I stalled, "why don't we go on over to your house now and get Mr. Brewer. I'll follow you."

"Oh, no, dear," she laughed. "I don't drive. I walked to town this morning and took the bus in."

"Where is the nearest bus station?" I asked. I had never seen buses anywhere *near* the funeral home.

"About two miles from here."

"Two miles!" I nearly shouted.

She laughed again. "That's nothing. When I was a little girl I used to walk over five miles to school—"

I gently cut her off. "Mrs. Brewer. Why don't we ride on over now and get Mr. Brewer. I'll make arrangements at your house and my colleagues can bring Mr. Brewer back here."

She frowned. "I don't see what all the hurry is about."

I thought quickly. "I am just thinking of the ants. Keep him safe from those ants."

She smiled. She liked that idea. "Okay. Let's do it. Can I ride with you or do I have to take the bus back?"

I laughed. "You can ride with me. Hang tight here and I'll be right back."

I went and got one of my colleagues from the never-ending meeting and, in hushed tones, told him about the current situation. He nearly yelled, "What?" down the hallway after I told him about Mr. Brewer, Mrs. Brewer, the bus, and the ants.

I called the Medical Examiner's office and asked them what they wanted to do. The deputy examiner told me she'd call me back.

We drove over to the Brewer house in two vehicles (fuel efficiency be damned, Howdy Doody). On the way over I received a call from the deputy examiner; she had sent a paramedic over so the death could be pronounced. She had talked to Mr. Brewer's doctor's office and his death wasn't unexpected. He was eighty-one, after all.

The Brewer house turned out to be a small cabin on the river, about three miles from the closest town. We had to wait a few minutes for the paramedic to show up and hook Mr. Brewer up to a wireless EKG machine so a physician at the closest hospital could pronounce his death. My co-worker and I performed the removal and then I sent Mr. Brewer off with my colleague while I stayed to make arrangements with Mrs. Brewer.

It was unseasonably clear and sunny for this part of Oregon. Mrs. Brewer invited me out to sit on their deck that overlooked the river and offered me a drink. I declined. She brought out a large glass pitcher of iced tea anyway. Real brewed, she informed me, complete with slices of lemon floating among the ice. How could I pass it up? Birds chirped and swatches of sunlight managed to penetrate the great leafy barrier above us as the sound of the river coursed softly in the background. It was a magnificent morning.

"Jim loved it here," Mrs. Brewer informed me, breaking my reverie. I noticed she had poured me the glass of tea. I sipped it. "We moved here from Maryland after his first heart attack in the late '70s. He just couldn't take the stress of litigation anymore. So we moved out here, he lost forty pounds, and we both learned to enjoy the simple life."

"You'll miss him, huh?"

"I will, but I won't. Jim is all around me...here. This place gave me another twenty years with him."

"I understand," I said, but in fact I didn't understand her not missing her husband. Her acceptance of his death and her total peace were puzzling to me.

"After he's laid out so our few friends and acquaintances can come pay their respects, I want him cremated so I can pour his ashes on the land he loved...the land that gave him—and me—his life back."

I stared at her, waiting for her to go on. She did.

"We had the cars. The money. The clothes. But that's about it. We didn't realize it at the time—you know—what we were missing. When we moved to Oregon we found that the void was our relationship. Out here we discovered the simple joys of just living an unhurried life, together. Jim and I created a world out here where money is of little consequence and folks don't call each other after regular business hours."

Taking another drink of iced tea, I realized she was right about what really matters. After that, whenever Howdy Doody tormented us with his boring rants, I pictured myself on Mrs. Brewer's porch, enjoying the tranquility of nature's beauty.

CHAPTER 6

Grandma Talk-Talk

Contributed by an entrepreneur

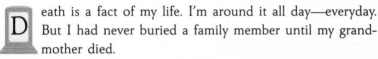eath is a fact of my life. I'm around it all day—everyday. But I had never buried a family member until my grandmother died.

When she passed away my relationship with death shifted from professional detachment to real human grief. Burying my grandmother was a strange and humbling experience. And, surprisingly, it was my grandmother who got me through it.

Grandma Talk-Talk helped raise my sister and me and was a real presence in our lives. She did all those grandmotherly things like letting us stay up late (blazing a trail of candy wrappers across her nice rugs), and slipping us a one-dollar bill to spend on even more candy. But she also did things that I didn't understand until much later.

She encouraged me to pursue my dreams. When I told her I wanted to be a funeral director, I can still hear her saying to me, "Kenny, open up your own mortuary. I know you can do it. Make something of yourself. You'll never go anywhere working for someone else."

I took her advice and now own a successful mortuary.

My sister, as a five-year-old, said about our grandmother, "all she does is talk, talk, talk...," hence the nickname. Grandma Talk-Talk had the same soft accent as Blanche on the Golden Girls—but Grandma Talk-Talk had more bite. There was a crispness to her speech that matched her dry humor. She danced with elegant, lightning speed from one subject to the next, wasting no time on breathing. Her "talkees" never stood a chance of talking.

When the mortuary phone rang and it was Grandma Talk-Talk, I knew I had to clear my schedule for at least an hour. I'd hear what food is being served in the retirement community; what birds she spotted that morning; what those "scoundrel Republicans" were up to; and the line she never failed to say, "Kenny, when I die, I want you to take care of me. I don't want some stranger who won't do nearly the job you do. You promise?" That request always made me uncomfortable, but, luckily, I knew she'd change the subject fast.

Burying a family member was still an abstract concept to me. Friends and neighbors, sure, but *family?* I figured that Grandma Talk-Talk had always been there—and would always continue to be there.

Then the day came when I felt for the first time that she wouldn't always be around. Her retirement home called my mortuary: Grandma was in the healthcare center and was fading fast.

Her retirement community is a seven hour drive south from where I live. With a cot and my dog, Roxy, I reluctantly set off. After Roxy and I were on the interstate for a bit, I started to notice the pavement whizzing by, butterflies collecting in my stomach, and I felt an uncontrollable urge to turn around. Instead of running away, though, I took deep breaths and slowed down. I wasn't sure I was ready to do this, but knew I had to. I was about to provide a woman who gave me so many gifts with the last gift I could give her.

I thought about trips to the beach with my sister and Grandma Talk-Talk. Grandma Talk-Talk in the driver's seat with no regard to (minimum) speed limits. Her giant boat of a Cadillac with its enormous front bench seat that the three of us shared, inching at 7mph while she talked nonstop. My sister and I hanging our heads out the window like happy summer dogs.

I dreaded the next few days. It would be so quiet. I had never been with my grandmother without her talk-talk. Roxy sat on the passenger seat, staring at me. She liked to stick her head out the window during car rides but, despite my offering a rolled-down window several times, today she just sat still.

By the time I arrived, Grandma Talk-Talk was dead.

My mother and sister greeted me at the door of her room.

"Kenny," my mom said, coming to hug me, "Grandma Talk-Talk is gone."

I nodded, didn't say anything, and opened the door. The lights were off but it was bright and sunny in her room. In the air hung the heavy smell of disinfectant and death. Dust motes swirled in the shafts of sunlight. Her oxygen machine had been unplugged and unhooked. The room was silent. I have seen thousands of dead people during the course of my career. This was the only one I can recall fearing to see.

I crept up to the bed and pulled down the sheet covering the still form. Grandma Talk-Talk looked peaceful, like she was asleep. Looking at her wasn't as bad as I had imagined. She almost looked like she was smirking in her sleep. I breathed a sigh of relief and pulled the sheet back over her face.

My sister took Roxy for a walk while I performed my job. I didn't want to dally; I had another job to do back at the mortuary. Thirty minutes after I pulled into the retirement community, I drove out of the parking lot yelling to my mom and sister, "I'll call you tomorrow!"

Roxy knew something was amiss. She lay down on the front seat and covered her head with her paw, something I had never seen her do before. The light was low as dusk set, and I headed for home with my dead grandma in the back.

I flipped on the radio to try to fill the void, but no matter how loud I turned the volume, it couldn't cover the *lack* of her talking. I sighed, turned the radio off, and rode in deafening silence.

As I hit a beltway and merged into rush-hour traffic, my grandma's voice popped into my head. "Kenny, take the HOV lane. You're allowed. We've got three!"

"What the hell," I muttered.

The silence wasn't so bad as I hurtled down the HOV lane reminiscing with Grandma Talk-Talk.

CHAPTER 7

A Case of Mistaken Identity

Contributed by a Red Sox fan

I work in a business traditionally recognized as a man's trade, and though I'm just a little girl playing in the big boy's club, I can handle it. I'm a Southie. And Southies are tough as nails.

Where I come from in south Boston, each group sticks to its own kind. It's more a matter of comfort level than prejudice against another ethnicity. The Jews go to the Jewish undertaker, the blacks go to the black undertaker, the Asians to the Asian, and so on. The undertakers for each group are familiar with the customs, rituals, and procedures at their places of worship.

At our company, we service the Irish Catholics. That's it. Don't get me wrong. Every once in a blue moon we work with a family that's Italian Catholic, Irish Protestant or even Russian Orthodox, and we are glad to provide them service. It's just a simple fact that when a family picks up the phone to dial the undertaker, they usually dial the firm down the street, not the one across town.

I was born to second-generation immigrants. My grandparents came from the town of Carrick-on-Shannon in the county Leitrim in the late '40s following the war and settled on the west side of south Boston. My grandfather worked as a machinist and my grandmother was a housekeeper. My grandfather is retired but still drinks full-time and my grandmother hasn't missed a day of work in almost twenty years. My father, whom I have never met, is rumored to have dealings with the IRA. He disappeared before I was born—a deadbeat (I'll leave out the adjectives I normally use). My mother worked for a meat packer for several years before landing herself in jail when I was five years old. I don't remember anything from when she was around other than the beautiful steaks we ate every night in our dingy little apartment. After my mother went away, I moved in with my grandparents and they raised me.

I went to work for an Irish-Catholic funeral home right out of mortuary school. I was the first woman funeral director they ever had in their fifty-plus esteemed years of business. I had it easy in some respects because the men went out of their way to help the "helpless" woman, but in other respects I had it much harder. I had a lot to prove in the all-boys club.

One morning, when I was as fresh in the business as a newborn babe in the woods, Kevin, the supervisor of the funeral home, came charging down the hall. "Katie!" he shouted. "I need you to head up to Lawrence today and pick up a trade job we got in last night." Kevin never *speaks*; he shouts.

"Who got it?" I inquired.

"The firm we always use up there." He looked at me like I was stupid, and his nose glowed like a red turnip on his flat face. "Turnbull Funeral Home." Kevin, though a blunderbuss, dresses impeccably, and on this day, already had his custom-made Cambridge suit jacket off and had sweated completely through his shirt. He's a real sweaty type guy.

"Oh," I said. I had been there once before and didn't realize Turnbull was the one we *always* used. But I kept quiet about that and filed that tidbit of information away. "You have the information?"

"Here it is," he said, pressing a slip of paper into my hand along with a twenty-dollar bill. "For tolls," he explained and winked.

Though Kevin sometimes has the temperament of a hibernating bear that has been woken, he can be a real sweetheart, too. "Thanks, Kevin," I said. "You're a doll." We both knew that as soon as I pulled out of the funeral home, I'd be pulling into the 7-Eleven to fortify myself with cigarettes and coffee.

He smiled at the praise and his bulbous nose wrinkled.

I loaded up the mini-van with a cot and was off, after stopping at 7-Eleven of course. The funeral home I work for sits outside of the city of Boston in one of the many suburbs, so when a death call comes in late at night from somewhere as far away as Lawrence, we call the local undertaker in that area to do the removal and, if necessary, embalming. There's no sense tying one of our directors up for three or more hours in the middle of the night, especially if we had a house call come in; the director on-call would have no way of getting back in time to make a speedy removal. Besides, the funeral home we use up in that area knows the hospital procedures, and can do the removal much more efficiently.

The drive took me the better part of an hour, during which I smoked damn near half the pack out of sheer boredom. I drove into the circular drive of the converted Victorian mansion and pulled around back. The grounds lining the drive were immaculate and I wouldn't be surprised if they had a full-time groundskeeper.

I backed the van onto the ramp leading down into the basement and hopped out. After popping into the office to let them know I was there, I went and waited by the van. One of their directors, the young guy I met last time I had been there, appeared. "Hi Charlie!" I said, perking up. I had the biggest crush on him. He was about my age—22—and looked like he played football in high school. I love burly guys.

"Hi." He flashed me a smile. "What's your name again?"

I was crestfallen. "Katie," I replied. We had had at least a twenty-minute conversation the last time I had been to Turnbull. Obviously, I hadn't plied my charms as well as I thought.

"Oh right," he said. "Who you here for?"

I didn't want to talk about that. I wanted to talk about giving him my phone number. But instead, the only thing that came out was, "Mrs. Walters."

He made a face. "Oh," he muttered, "I got her last night. What a night."

I changed the subject to something flirtier as I unloaded the cot from the van and followed him down the ramp.

He didn't take the conversational bait. He was only interested in business. "Here she is," he said and peeled back a sheet covering one of the many bodies in the morgue, just enough so the wrist tag could be read. I noted Mrs. Walters was a very handsome looking African-American woman, but I was too busy sweet-talking Charlie to glance at the tag. I just nodded.

He lowered the sheet.

I was grabbing at straws. I had already been through weather, traffic, and work. "Sorry we got you out of bed last night," I said and I cringed hearing my own cheesy laugh.

Charlie made another face. "Yeah, thanks."

I grinned.

"Let's get her moved over." Charlie consulted his watch. "I have a wake that's wrapping up in twenty minutes."

Damn, he's too preoccupied with his service to think about me, I thought dejectedly.

We transferred Mrs. Walters and I was on my way without Charlie's phone number. Next time, I promised myself. I really needed to meet Charlie somewhere more conducive to flirting than a morgue, though I wasn't sure how I was going to orchestrate it. Wasn't like I was going to run into him at the neighborhood pub. I smoked the other half of the pack of cigarettes on the return trip and tried to formulate a plan.

When I arrived at my funeral home I unloaded Mrs. Walters and wheeled her into our morgue. "Hey, Kevin," I called, running after him as he charged up the hall.

"Everything go all right?" he called over his shoulder, not stopping but slowing down.

He was getting to the point in the day where his neatly pressed clothes had long since lost their crispness.

I shrugged. "Yeah. Fine. This is the first black woman we've had since I've been here."

He stopped in the hallway, turned and just stared at me. His face was bright red. "McCullough, you dumbass!" he exploded. "You got the wrong person!"

I froze. "Huh?" I replied dumbly. A million thoughts raced through my head. I hadn't been cautious and checked the tags as I should have. I had been too busy flirting. Charlie had given me the wrong person! "Are you sure?"

"Yes!" he screamed. "I just met with the family. They're white! Now get her back to that funeral home and get the right person before we all lose our licenses!" He turned heel and stomped toward his office, cursing under his breath.

I ran into the morgue and ripped the sheet off and checked Mrs. Walters's hospital ID bracelet—the end-all of identification. I read it and re-read the name—Joanne Walters. They had mislabeled her.

I raced into his office. "Kevin, the hospital mislabeled her! Maybe the real Mrs. Walters is still at the hospital morgue."

He stared at me with his beady eyes. Behind his desk he looked like a big red toad, all puffed up and furious.

"I'm serious. The bracelet says—" I trailed off feebly.

Kevin got up, glaring at me, and stalked out of his office.

I went to follow but he held up a pudgy finger indicating for me to wait. A few seconds later, after what seemed like an eternity, Kevin came back chuckling. "That's her, all right," he said.

"What?" I said, confused. "I thought you said she's white."

"She is white."

"Huh?"

"Jaundice. It can sometimes give the skin a tint like that."

"Like that?" I was relieved and flabbergasted.

"You know how jaundice turns the skin yellow?" Kevin said, still laughing.

"Yeah."

"Well, sometimes the embalming fluid will react with the chemical that causes the jaundice and turn the skin other colors."

"Oh jeez, you nearly gave me a heart attack a minute ago," I said.

"You? What about the heart attack you nearly gave me!"

"I didn't mean to," I protested.

He laughed. "Rookie mistake. Hell, McCullough, get out of here. Go home and pour yourself a stiff drink. We'll chalk this one up to inexperience... and I won't tell the boys," he said, referring to the other men.

"Thanks," I said, really meaning it. "I don't think I'd ever live this one down."

"They were rookies at one point. We all were."

Though Kevin was trying to be nice, I was still mad at myself. A magician's sleight of hand involves using psychology to direct your eye one way while she or he manipulates the trick elsewhere. I performed a sleight of hand on myself; right before my own eyes, without realizing it, so engrossed was I with the less-fair sex.

The dead can't tell you who they are. That's my job: to know, to make sure, to double check, and to triple check. That day was an important lesson in doing my job. No matter what the job, do it right, and do it right the first time. No excuses.

Southies don't make excuses.

CHAPTER 8

Ousting the Coroner

Contributed by a college basketball fan

I used to contract with the county to do body removals for the coroner's office. When a death occurs outside of a normal setting like a hospital, convalescent home, or home hospice care, the coroner is called to investigate. His investigation of the scene determined where I took the body. If the coroner believed the death to be anything other than natural (or sometimes, accidental), I took the body back to his laboratory for an autopsy by a pathologist. If he ruled it to be a natural death, then I would take the body back to my funeral home, or another funeral home of the family's choosing, and things would proceed from there. The money was terrible, but it kept my fledgling business afloat through some rough patches in the early years.

Before the state allocated money for an official county coroner's building, the autopsies used to be performed at my funeral home. To my relief, the state later coughed up enough money so we no longer have to deal with our morgue being commandeered as a quasi-government facility. The pathologist always left a mess.

It can be a raw job at times—doing removals for the coroner. I've been summoned at all hours of the night, to all kinds of places, and seen bodies in all kinds of conditions, in all types of weather. The coroner doesn't get called if some sweet, old lady dies of heart failure at home under hospice care. No, the coroner gets called when there's a mess to be cleaned up. When he got called, I got called.

I can't tell you how many times I've been called to the scene of a car wreck and lined the body bags up along the shoulder of the road while deputies and firemen collected the body parts, or been called to a homicide so recent that the blood hasn't had time to congeal—the sweet smell of iron hanging heavy in the air. The suicides made me introspective and the freak accidents made me believe in Existentialism, but they all made me just a little bit more jaded. I had the contract with the county for seven years before the strain of the work became too much and I called it quits. The tragedy of all those shattered human beings drained me emotionally and physically.

These days I'm happy to sit in my big-cheese office, in my fine suits, and go about my business in a relaxed fashion while some other hungry upstart funeral director deals with the dirty job of doing removals for the coroner's office. I saw a lot of things during those seven years, but the removal that I remember most happened the first year I held the contract.

My funeral home wasn't doing very many calls a year. One weekday morning I was drinking coffee and reading the sports scores when the phone rang. It was the coroner's office; a body had been found in the foothills. I took the location from the woman, thanked her, and hung up. I called a part-time guy, Paul, who helped me do removals, and he agreed to me meet me at the funeral home.

We piled into the run-out old Chevy station wagon and drove out to the site. I live near the foothills of the Sierra Nevada Mountains. The weather fronts that blow off the Pacific Ocean hit the mountains and have nowhere to go, so they dump their precipitation. It's usually raining in my neck of the woods. This day was no exception. It was more like a heavy mist than an actual rain, but combined with the chilly air, it was a certifiable foul day. One of the sheriff's deputies recognized my vehicle as we pulled up to the scene and waved us through the cones he had set up on the lonely mountain road.

I stepped out of the wagon and turned my collar up. It was no use; the wind still cut right through the fabric. The area where the body had been found was on a bend of a secondary road leading up towards the mountains. Old-growth forest towered over the road on one side, and on the other, an embankment dropped away from the road. I walked over to the guardrail where the coroner was staring down the hill intently.

"Hey, Joe," I said, fumbling for my cigarettes in my pocket with frozen fingers.

He glanced at me, grunted, cigar clamped between his lips, and then looked back down the hill.

I pulled out a cigarette and inserted it between my lips. "Nasty fall, huh?" I said, following his gaze down the steep embankment to where I could see two deputies picking their way through the brush around the little stream at the bottom of the ravine.

Joe grunted again, and pulled his cigar from his lips with his thick fingers.

I tried lighting a match but the moisture just made it crumble. I tried several before I gave up and flicked my unlit cigarette down the hill in disgust. "So, what's the story?"

Joe sneered. "What does it look like?" he said. "Asshole fell. Got what he deserved for walking around here at night. No streetlights out here in the boondocks."

I stared down the muddy embankment to the little creek that had formed at the bottom of the ravine and wished I hadn't worn one of my few suits. I knew this wouldn't be a tidy job.

"Hey fellas! Find anything down there?" Joe yelled.

The deputies at the bottom of the ravine looked up and shook their heads. Not that they were really looking any too hard for clues. They were pussyfooting around in the tall grass, trying to steer clear of the mud and water.

"Well, Toules, looks like we have an obvious accident on our hands." Joe pushed up off the guardrail where he had been resting his foot, using his knee as a leaning post.

"You going to go down and look for yourself?" I asked, incredulous. Joe was lazy and had the kind of stupidity combined with cunning intellect that could get you in trouble if you crossed him. He had been elected into office eons ago, and just kept getting re-elected. It was almost like he got recycled in spite of himself. The more he got re-elected the lazier he got.

"I can see just fine from up here what happened. Obvious accident."

I squinted down into the ravine. "You sure?" I asked dubiously.

"Fell."

"He fell *over* the guardrail?"

Joe took the stub out of his mouth and flicked it at my feet. "What? You want to play coroner today, Toules? My job here is done. You and your corpse-humping friend get your asses down there and drag that body out of that water, and try not to get your nice shoes wet." He pounded me on the back and laughed meanly. "I'll stop over later to make an ID," he called over his shoulder.

Asshole, I thought, as Joe got into his government-issue sedan and took off with a squeal of tires.

"Does he do anything?" Paul asked as I returned to the wagon.

"No, except stuff his face at Smiley's Diner."

We both laughed.

"Lets get this over with," I said and sighed.

"Bad?" Paul asked.

"It's going to be messy."

I put on a pair of rubbers to protect my good shoes and donned a pair of large yellow kitchen gloves, the kind that go nearly up to your elbow. We used them for coroner-related work because we never knew what kind of mess we'd find, and they afforded a little more protection than regular latex gloves. Paul pulled the cot out onto the pavement and collapsed it to the ground. I got out a black body bag and a coil of rope. Handing the coil of rope to my partner, I hopped over the guardrail and wind-milled my arms as I slid down the muddy slope. Thankfully, I made it to the bottom without falling. Paul wasn't so lucky.

I found myself standing in sixteen inches of muddy water and him sitting in it. We turned the air blue with our language as we got to work. I unfolded the thick vinyl body bag on the tall grass of the stream's embankment parallel to the facedown man.

We both stood in the stream. I grabbed the arms, Paul took the legs, and we hoisted him right out of the stream and into the bag. I zipped it up, and we flipped the body bag over so we didn't drag the man facedown. Paul looped the rope through one of the sturdy nylon handles and climbed the ravine hill. He slipped a couple of times, and each time a loud cuss word cut through the si-lent mountain air like the report of a gunshot. When Paul made it to the top of the embankment, he looped the rope around the guardrail. Then he pulled on the rope as I grabbed a handle and helped drag the body bag back across the stream and up the muddy hill.

Paul and I loaded the body bag onto the cot and put it in the back of the station wagon. We waved to the deputies and sped off.

Hours later, after I had time to change out of my ruined suit, shoes, and raincoat, Paul and I stood in the morgue and placed the body bag on the porcelain embalming table. Since the zipper was on the underside of the man, I took a pair of shears and cut the bag down the center.

We stepped back in surprise, and I think Paul captured both our feelings with two words. He covered his mouth with his gloved hand and whispered, "Oh, shit!"

The man lay on the table, staring up at us with surprised, vacant eyes. A ten-inch piece of chrome bumper stuck out from his torso. Clearly, he had been the victim of a hit-and-run.

I was on the phone to the state within minutes. Coroner Joe offered his resignation less than a week later.

CHAPTER 9

Spare Donuts

Contributed by a Brazilian Jiu-Jitsu fighter

W hen I was in mortuary school my roommate was raped. I took to carrying pepper spray in my pocketbook for protection, which in hindsight would've been as effective as trying to use a garden hose to put out a forest fire. By the time I had identified the danger, dug around all the junk in my purse looking for the darn can, and then figured out how to point and spray, I would have been a goner. But it made me feel safe at the time. After college I was looking for a hobby, something to unwind from work, and started doing Brazilian Jiu-Jitsu, partly to learn something new, partly because I like to exercise, and partly to replace my can of pepper spray.

Jiu-Jitsu is a martial art used by ancient Samurai warriors. It uses punches, kicks, throws, and ground grappling. Brazilian Jiu-Jitsu is a derivative of it that focuses more on takedowns and ground grappling than its counterpart. Over 90 percent of street fights end on the ground, so it's imperative that you know how to get your opponent on the ground and then control him. I don't go around looking for fights. I'm just comfortable in situations where most women wouldn't be...like stranded on the side of Interstate 25 in the dark with a van full of dead bodies.

I work for a mortuary near Santa Fe. People who aren't familiar with the area would have no idea where my hometown is, so
I just tell everyone "Santa Fe." It's a quaint little town sitting on
the edge of the desert framed by the Sangre de Cristo Mountains.
I've lived in the Southwest my entire life and would never dream
of moving. I love it too much.

We were quite busy at work one day with three funerals, and
during the course of the day two calls came in from Albuquerque,
which is only about an hour away. It's not uncommon for calls
to come from families with loved ones at Albuquerque-area hospitals because they have excellent care facilities and some of the
most advanced trauma units for hundreds of miles.

It was early evening in the wintertime, so it was getting dark
when I loaded up the panel van with a cremation box. I was going
to stop on the way back from Albuquerque at our retort—the
technical term for a cremation chamber—that's across town and
then drop the body off. It would be ready to be cremated first
thing the following morning. The van has two steel shelves built
in, almost like the old World War I ambulances, so that up to
four bodies can be carried at once. With the help of one of my
co-workers, I put the box on one of the shelves, loaded two empty
cots, and headed out.

I made good time going to Albuquerque because all the rush
hour traffic was heading out of the city as I was heading in. I
stopped at Presbyterian Hospital and picked up the first body,
and then stopped at UNM Hospital and picked up the second.
Because it was after hours and I had to wait for security to key
me into the morgues, it took about two hours to get both bodies. At this point it was near 8:30 and I was starved, so I stopped
at a café and parked the van out front where I could see it while
I grabbed a quick bite to eat. I did some quick time calculations
in my head and called my boyfriend.

I told him I was running a little late, and probably wouldn't
be home until ten o'clock or so, and asked him if he could give

the babysitter a ride home. Freddie, like me, sometimes works late. He told me he was just leaving the office. We exchanged "I love you's" and hung up.

I hopped back in the van, wanting to get home to Freddie and my daughter as soon as possible. I navigated back onto I-25 and headed north. I was doing a pretty good clip when I hit some road debris. The van jolted so hard I looked in the rearview mirror to see what I had hit. I couldn't tell what it was. *No matter,* I thought, and quickly forgot. About five more miles down the highway I heard a noise. It got louder until it sounded like a helicopter was hovering over me. When the tire exploded it sounded like a bomb going off.

The van swerved wildly, but I managed to keep control of it and pulled off to the side of the interstate. I got out and inspected the left front tire. It was totally shredded. There was almost no rubber left on the smoking rim. *This is just great!* I kicked the side of the van in frustration. *There goes my Q.T. with Freddie tonight!*

I retrieved my cell phone from inside and called an emergency roadside assistance company. The dispatcher notified me help was on the way, and advised me to hang tight. I hung up and got back into the nice warm van. While I waited, I called my partner at the mortuary and told him the situation, and that I'd probably be an hour late. The original plan was for me to get the bodies from the hospital and he was going to embalm them. Upon hearing that I wouldn't be back at the mortuary until eleven o'clock, he told me to leave them and he'd take care of them in the morning.

Bored, I flipped through the radio stations for almost an hour before a pair of headlights pulled up behind me. I hopped out into the freezing desert air and ran to the rear of the van, hugging my wool coat tight around me. The figure in the white pickup truck engaged an emergency light bar over the cab of his truck and got out. He was an elderly gentleman, probably working during his retirement years to stay busy.

"Hey there," I greeted him. He clutched a couple of road flares in his hand.

"Hull-o, Miss," he replied. "I understand you have a blowout?"

"Yeah. Left front tire is completely gone."

He smiled at me with crooked teeth. He wasn't wearing much more than a heavy flannel shirt and a ball cap. He was the type accustomed to working outdoors in the cold. "We'll have you underway in just a few minutes, Miss." He popped the flares and dropped them on the rumble strip alongside the van.

"Oh, thank you, sir," I said. "It's been a long day and I'm ready to get home."

"Let's have a look." He loped up to the front of the van and poked at the tire. "Yup. Blew it out all right. Thankfully you didn't bend the rim, so everything is going to be fine. You probably won't need a tow unless you bent the axle."

I breathed a sigh of relief.

"Seems to me, if I remember correctly, the spare for this is located behind the front seats in the cargo area under the floorboards."

"Okay," I said and swung the doors open.

The man peered into the cargo area. "What's that?" he asked and put a crooked finger on his grizzled chin.

"Just a couple of bodies," I said briskly. "I'll move them out of the way so you can get to the tire."

The man recoiled. "I'm not touching this van!"

"What?" I said, confused. "Don't be ridiculous. I'll pull the bodies out and you do your job. You don't have to touch them."

"I'm not getting in there!" he said. "There are dead people in there!"

My gratitude quickly melted into frustration. "Then what are you here for if you're not going to help me?"

"I'm not getting anywhere near no dead people." He took a step backward toward his pickup.

I snorted. "Then just get the hell out of here! I'll do it myself,"

I yelled. I had never changed a tire before on a car, much less a giant van, but I wasn't going to sit around and suffer this fool.

I pulled the two cots out onto the shoulder of the freeway. The cars zipping by slowed; a strange scene was unfolding on the side of the road and the drivers wanted to rubberneck. I crawled into the back of the van, lifted up the floorboard, and retrieved the spare tire and jack. The tire didn't look like the regular ones. It was smaller and didn't look as sturdy—almost like a donut.

I rolled the donut between the suspended steel bays and crawled out, my charcoal pantsuit pants now smeared and greasy. I noticed with annoyance the guy was sitting in his pickup, watching. I loaded the two cots back inside the van and marched back to the pickup and rapped on the window. He rolled his window down.

"There," I said, "the bodies are all gone, now do your job."

He looked at me and said, "I told you I'm not going near that death van."

"Then go on. Get the hell out of here. I don't need you if you aren't going to do anything."

"Can't. Gotta stay. Rules."

"Do the rules also mention you sitting on your ass doing nothing?" I glared at him and marched back to the spare and jack. I picked them up and went around to the front of the van and got down on my hands and knees and looked under the chassis of the van. I found what appeared to me to be a suitable place to put the jack and started cranking. After I had the rim off the ground a few inches, I took the wrench and tugged at the bolts holding the old tire on.

"You're doing it wrong!" the man called from his truck. I ignored him. The bolts were stiff and I was using every ounce of my strength. The van rocked perilously. I stopped and waited for it to stop moving. Then I tugged at the wrench, applying more even force. *These bolts are really on there,* I thought as I gave the wrench a final pull. The jack kicked out from under the van and it crashed down. I dove out of the way just in time. I sat on my rear end a few feet away, shaking from my close call.

"You've got to loosen the lugs before you jack up the van!" the man in the pickup truck called.

Thanks, asshole! I thought, picking myself up off the shoulder and dusting my coat off.

I retrieved the wrench from where I had flung it and found that by partially standing, I could put all my weight into loosening the bolts. I got all five loose and again jacked up the van. I slipped the spare on the rim and let the vehicle down. The spare donut seemed really soft, but I wasn't going to ask the useless idiot in the pickup for anything like an air pump.

I tightened the bolts and navigated slowly back onto the interstate. Opening my window, I flipped the old guy the bird before I roared off. I kept the van at thirty-five all the way to the mortuary.

It was a long ride back.

CHAPTER 10

Severe Clear

Contributed by a bicyclist

O ne night about ten years ago, I received a call at the witching hour. It's not at all unusual in my business to get calls in the middle of the night, but this call was quite unusual. It went something like this:

"Freeman Mortuary. Gabe speaking."

"Yes," the shaky voice on the other end of the line said. "My name is Betty Drake. I'm sorry to bother you but I didn't know who else to call." She paused and wept.

"Did someone pass away?" I inquired, still lying in bed with my wife, the lights out.

"Yes...no. It's our dog, Clear."

"Oh," I replied. "I'm so sorry to hear that."

"Thank you," Betty said. "We heard some noises about an hour ago and came out to the kitchen—my husband and I—and found him...dead!" She wept again. I remained silent. Betty composed herself and continued. "We just moved here and we didn't know who to call. My husband suggested I look in the phone book for a funeral home. We knew the undertaker where we used to live and he came and got our last dog twelve years ago. I found your number in the Yellow Pages and called."

"You want me to come get your dog?" I asked.

"Well, yes," she said. "If that's something you do."

No, that's not something I do, I thought, *but what the hell.* "I'd be happy to come get your dog," I said. "What kind is it?"

She told me and gave me her address. I promised to be there within the hour and hung up. I redialed the phone. "Hey, Tom, don't be mad, but—"

When I hung up with Tom, I lay in bed for a moment thinking, *Don't look at the clock, don't look at the clock.* I looked and groaned. My wife just rolled over and continued sleeping.

Tom and I arrived at the Drake household forty-five minutes later and found a crying Mrs. Drake and a somber Mr. Drake. They were an older couple; I guessed them to be in their early to mid-sixties. Mrs. Drake led us into the kitchen, where one of the most beautiful dogs I have ever seen, a husky with a black and white coat lay on the floor.

"We were never able to have children," Mrs. Drake said. "So our dogs are like—" She bit her sentence off.

Mr. Drake knelt next to the dog and stroked the fur around his neck. "You ever dive?"

"Excuse me?" I said, confused.

"Dive. You know, skydive?"

"No," I said, "can't say that I have." I was lost.

"We called him Clear," he said. "His official name on his kennel papers is Severe Clear because his eyes were the exact color of the sky on a perfect skydiving day, called a severe clear day." Not sure if I was supposed to comment, I remained silent. "I was Airborne. I used to dive," Mr. Drake said, looking up for the first time from his place on the floor.

I nodded.

"I dove for sport later in life. When Betty brought this little guy home from the kennel and I saw those eyes, I knew exactly what we were going to name him. Either of you guys have dogs?"

Tom and I nodded. Tom has a chocolate Lab, and I have a Yorkshire terrier, so we know what it's like to be attached to a dog. People who don't have pets don't realize what a big presence they are in the house, but they each have their own personalities. They become part of the family.

We expressed our sympathies to the Drakes and Mr. Drake escorted the still crying Mrs. Drake out of the kitchen while we loaded the eighty-pound husky onto the cot and took him back to the funeral home. The Drakes stood on the front stoop and watched as we pulled away. Mrs. Drake hugged herself while Mr. Drake stood with his arm around his wife's shoulders.

The next day I took Clear to the animal crematorium, and later in the week transferred his ashes from the little plastic box that held his remains to a small blue painted steel urn.

I got busy, and it was two weeks before I was able to deliver the urn to Mrs. Drake. When she saw the urn with the name Severe Clear on the brass nameplate, she started to cry. "I thought the color was fitting," I told her.

She just nodded through her tears. Finally, she regained her composure enough to ask, "How much do I owe you?"

"Nothing. Just count this as a favor from one dog owner to another."

"Thank you so much," she gushed. "Could I invite you in?" I declined, saying I was busy. As I turned to leave, Mrs. Drake said, "We miss him so much, you know. Thank you from the bottom of my heart, Gabe. You have made this really easy."

I thanked her for her kind words and bid her goodbye, and chalked the whole thing up to good karma.

Now, I'm not trying to toot my own horn, telling people they'll "get something" for doing a good deed. I certainly wasn't looking to get anything from the Drakes. But in the ten years that have elapsed since I went to their household in the middle of the night to get Severe Clear, both of Mrs. Drake's parents have died and she called me, remembering my kindness. And recently, when Mr. Drake died, Mrs. Drake called me to take care of him. We placed the blue urn in his casket.

"It just seems fitting," Mrs. Drake said.

I agreed.

CHAPTER 11

Roadblock

Contributed by a retired infantry officer

I grew up in the city. My favorite time of year is winter. There is nothing more beautiful than a snowy cityscape. The whiteness blankets the filth and urban ugliness with cleanliness and soft edges while the urbanites run for the shelter of their giant buildings, leaving the streets deserted. The only problem is that the snow makes my job damn near impossible to do, or so I found out the hard way one night when I nearly quit, but I'll get to that later.

I was a career infantry officer in the Army. Got commissioned as a 2nd lieutenant, saw some combat, got decommissioned with silver oak leaves—a light colonel. I traveled around the world several times over and saw a lot of things. Some good. Some bad. But it was all interesting. My career propelled a troubled eighteen-year-old boy out of an equally troubled area, gave him an education, and gave him a life. I shudder to think what would have become of me if I hadn't joined the Army. I'd probably be in prison, or worse.

When I retired from the Army at age fifty-four I didn't know what to do with myself. I still got up at 5 A.M., I still kept my hair high and tight, and I still rolled my socks the Army way. It's hard to know what to do when nobody's giving you orders, if all you know is how to take orders. My wife finally shooed me out of the house. I was driving her crazy.

I took some classes, volunteered, and even tried a new hobby—watercolor. I found I hate watercolor. My colors always ran together and I all I ever got was a big brown mess and elevated blood pressure. The classes bored me, and the volunteering…let's just say I've found that I'm too old to change the world, or too tired. I can't decide. I was like a ship in a storm without a tiller.

Then my mother died and everything changed.

We called the undertaker my family has used in town for ages: Pickering and Sons, Inc. They came to my house, where my mother had been living with us, and did the removal. The next day I went in and met with the owner, Thomas F. Pickering, V, to make arrangements.

It wasn't a sad occasion. My mother was old, and it was her time. She had lived the hard life of a single parent, trying to feed herself and her son by cleaning hotel rooms. My wife and I were planning on burying her in the cemetery plot we were eventually planning to use ourselves. No fuss. No fanfare. I told Thomas Pickering my plans, and afterward we got to talking. I told him how as a boy, when I lived in the city near their old funeral home, I used to wash cars for his grandfather, Thomas F. Pickering, III, and do other little jobs to earn a bit of money to blow at the five-and-dime store. I then proceeded to tell Mr. Pickering how if I hadn't gotten into mischief and subsequently gone into the service to avoid jail time, I could easily have envisioned myself as an undertaker.

I was half joking.

"It's never too late," Mr. Pickering told me and handed me his card.

It was an impressive card, cream-colored linen stock with raised ink lettering bearing fancy script and the family crest.

"We use part-time employees all the time, and I'm always looking for reliable help."

"I don't know, sir—"

He interrupted. "Please. It's Tom."

I laughed. "Sorry. Force of habit. Back to what I was saying. I'll be pushing sixty real hard in a few years. I imagine you need strapping young recruits to do this job."

He shrugged. "Obviously you need to have some strength, but older guys can do it just as well. I've found that older people are much more reliable than the younger crowd. I call some twenty-something part-timer on a Friday evening and what's he tell me?"

"He's gotten into the sauce?"

"Exactly!" Tom exclaimed and pounded the desk. He stroked his silver goatee, looked at me, and winked. "Not that I don't like a pop every now and again, but you can't go pick up a body when you're drunk. It's not professional, and it's dangerous."

I was listening.

"Well, Nicholas, if you find you're ever interested in pursuing that second career, or just looking for something to keep you busy, give me a call. I'd be happy to add you to my roster. Besides," he said and gestured across his giant mahogany desk to me, "you don't give yourself enough credit. You look as fit and trim as any twenty-year-old who has ever worked here." And it was true that the Army had instilled in me a rigorous schedule of exercise that kept me limber and free of the paunch many of my peers were plagued with.

I placed his fancy card in my shirt pocket. We settled up the bill and later that week buried my mother.

Tom's card sat on my bureau for a couple of months. I suffered through some more interminable watercolor attempts and too many sessions of a dreary class at the senior learning center (a name I hate) called "Manifest Destiny: Land Bondage of the American Indians" before I mustered the courage to pick up the phone. Tom hired me right on the spot. Soon I was doing re-movals for the firm, a week on, a week off. When I am "on" I carry a pager with me twenty-four hours a day. Another gentleman and I work together, alternating. He does a removal and I do the next one. And if it is a residential removal, we both go together.

I finally had a mission!

The beauty of the job is that I can just get in the van and go, and there is enough work that it keeps me as busy as I want to be in my retirement years. Sometimes, they even send me on road trips to pick up or deliver a trade job (a body that's embalmed by another funeral director) or take a burial out of town in the hearse. I am in different places and situations every day, meeting people at every turn. It's certainly never dull, almost like being back in the good ol' Army.

The only time I almost quit was a couple of years ago right around Christmas. I was dispatched to a nursing home in the city. I hate doing removals there because of the parking problems, and to top it off it looked like it was going to be a white Christmas. It was snowing hard.

This particular nursing home was in an established residential section of the city, where there was just room enough for the building—nothing else—certainly no parking lot. The ambulance ramp at the rear of the building extends out to the sidewalk on a one-way street. Normally, this would worry me because I have to park in the middle of the street and block traffic, but the snow compounded my worries. Snow and ice make navigating the cot hard enough, but going down a slippery ramp with at least a hundred pounds of weight is a near-impossible feat. The only thing I had working in my favor was the fact that the call came in at eleven o'clock at night. That meant traffic would be light.

I got to the nursing home, parked the van in the middle of the street, and took the keys out, even though it was below freez-ing and I would have preferred to keep the heater running. I put the emergency flashers on, wheeled the cot up the ramp, and was buzzed in. A sleepy and slightly hostile nurse threw some papers in front of me and pointed me to Mrs. Jardeen's room. Much to my dismay, Mrs. Jardeen was, to put it nicely, a big woman. I hefted her onto the cot, pulled the straps tight, and headed back out into the tempest. The staff at the nursing home hadn't salted the ramp. Holding onto the rail with one hand and allowing the weight of the cot to pull me, I slowly slid down the ramp without incident.

I was so pleased with myself at successfully navigating the slushy ramp that I threw caution to the wind. Mistake. As I lowered one end of the cot off the curb it hit a patch of ice and swung wildly to the right. I desperately twisted the rear of the cot into the skid, trying to stop it, but the weight on the cot torqued it right out of my hands. The force I was using to pull the cot suddenly wasn't counter-balanced and I fell backward. I ended up sitting hard on my rear on the snowy sidewalk. The first thing out of my mouth was, "Oh, shit!" I watched in slow motion as the front wheels swung back to the curb and hit it. The forward momentum of Mrs. Jardeen kicked the legs of the cot out. It flopped on its side in a growing snow bank with a sickening *thump.*

I sat for a moment on the cold, snowy sidewalk, stupefied by the little drama that had just played out before my eyes. I finally got up and dusted myself off and tried hefting the cot up. She was far too heavy for me to dead lift—no pun intended. There I was, out on the deserted city street in the middle of the night with a flipped cot and my van blocking the road...in a snowstorm.

Making a quick decision, I ran back up the ramp and got re-buzzed in. I found the surly nurse and explained my situation to her.

She looked at me like I was crazy. "Honey," she said, "I just got off disability. There's no way I'm going out and lifting something heavy like that. Once Mrs. Jardeen went through that door she was no longer my responsibility."

"What?" I was incredulous that she could be that callous.

The nurse pursed her lips.

"Is there anyone in here that can help me?" I nearly screamed at her. I pounded on the counter, my eyes bulging. I stopped and collected myself.

The nurse didn't seem concerned. She pulled a strand of hair and looked at the ceiling, deep in thought. After an eternity she said, "Nah. I can't think of anyone on tonight that can help you."

Oh, great, I had visions of jumping over the countertop and wringing her apathetic neck.

"Oh, wait," she said. "Jamal, he can help you."

My spirits rose, but she quickly dashed them. "No, wait, he called in. Ain't coming in on account of the storm."

"Wonderful." I didn't know anyone in the city who could help me. I'd have to call my partner and wait for him to drive the twenty or so minutes. "Can I use your phone?" I asked.

When she offered it up, I nearly ripped it out of her hands. As I told the dispatcher at the funeral home what had happened, I heard him mutter, "Christ," under his breath. I wanted to strangle him. He was in his nice warm home sleeping and judging me! But I kept it together long enough to slam down the phone on him after he told me he'd put a call in to my partner.

I stalked back out to the van, so mad at myself I wanted to scream. I like things to work as planned. I think it's the Army in me. When I screw up and the plan goes awry, it makes me furious. There was nothing I could do at that point. So I did the only thing I could do for Mrs. Jardeen—I dusted off the snow that was accumulating on the cot cover and got in the van to wait for my partner.

Several cars pulled up behind me flashing their lights and honking, and each time I had to get out and tell them to back up and detour. I wasn't about to leave Mrs. Jardeen alone, even for a second. It took forty-five minutes for my partner to arrive due to the snow and ice. He later told me that he wanted to laugh, but after he saw the murderous look in my eye decided against it.

The next day Tom called me into his office. I thought for sure he was going to fire me, and to be perfectly honest, I was so embarrassed I wanted to quit.

"Nicholas," he said to me, "I heard about your little incident last night." He laced his fingers together and stuck them under his chin. His serious face melted into a mischievous smile. "Sounds like you had quite the little adventure in the city."

"Yes," I said, sitting rigid in the chair facing his desk. "It was an absolute nightmare."

He laughed.

"What?" I demanded.

"You should see your face!"

"What about it?"

"You're so serious." Tom was belly laughing. "I bet you were a sight to see last night. Blocking the street...body laying on the sidewalk...nurses basically telling you to go chase yourself." The laughter was shaking his entire body. "Nicholas, you're too serious."

"I like to be as professional as I can—"

Tom cut me off. "I can remember this one time I let a cot fall off a ramp into the bushes. The ramp had no railing and I drove the cot right over the edge." Tears were coming to his eyes. "A pebble got caught in the wheel and it turned suddenly and I basically lost control of it. Boy, was my father mad at me that day! Man, oh man. He wouldn't talk to me for the longest time. And you're sitting here all upset because you slipped on the ice. What? Did you think I was going to fire you?"

"Well, yeah—"

"Nicholas, you've got to lighten up a little. I realize you do your best all the time, but this job is so unpredictable you have to laugh sometimes or you'll cry. The important thing is you didn't hurt yourself last night. That nurse should be tied and quartered, but what can you do? Honestly, Nicholas, what can you do? You did the right thing, and that's all I can ask. I wish I had two more of you."

"Thanks. I guess," I said.

I left his office that day feeling puzzled but relieved. I did learn an important lesson about my limitations. Our motto in the 7th Infantry was *volens et potens*, willing and able. My new motto, a quote by Horace, is: *mors ultima linea rarum est*, death is everything's final limit. Working around death sure has showed me some of my own limitations.

And I still hate watercolor.

CHAPTER 12

Human Wedge

Contributed by a shameless karaoke singer

here do most unexpected home deaths occur? Think about it. The bathroom. Picture this: you're not feeling well, so you get out of bed or your comfy chair and when you stand up, the feeling persists. You can't put your finger on it, but the uneasiness is spreading. Something just isn't right. What do you do? You head for the nearest bathroom, moving as fast as you can. Something is *really* not right. You walk through the bathroom door and keel over, dead.

I have hauled countless people out of bathtubs, off toilets, and off the bathroom floor over the years, all to the same tune of the spouse in the background saying, "I don't know what happened. He/she was fine last night. I heard him/her get up and get a drink of water around midnight, and then I found him/her like this in the morning." It's always the same story, different bathroom.

The one incident I vividly remember is when I went in to do a removal, not through the bathroom door, but through a hole chopped in the side of the house.

An elderly gentleman lived alone. After a few days of not seeing the man, and the newspapers piling up, a concerned neighbor keyed herself in. The gentleman's keys were on the kitchen counter as was his wallet, and there was a strange smell coming from his bathroom. The woman called out but got no answer. After trying the knob and finding it unlocked, she tried pushing on the door. It was jammed, as if a large weight was lying on the other side. Fearing for her friend's safety, the woman dialed 9-1-1.

The police and firemen showed up. After some investigation, one of the cops, a friend of mine, called me to get over to the house. "I know decomp when I smell it," he said. Decomp is short for decomposition. "I know he's dead in there. The old guy must've had a heart attack in the bathroom and fallen against the door."

"Family?" I inquired.

"Didn't have any. I'm calling on behalf of the neighbor lady. She told me she's going to be making the arrangements."

"M.E.?"

"Medical Examiner already called the doctor. They don't want the case. Old guy had a long history of heart problems. He was a ticking time bomb. Once we get him out and the paramedics pronounce, he'll be all yours."

"Be right over," I said.

I puttered over in my hearse at my leisure. I knew it would be a while before the firemen took the door off its hinges and the paramedics pronounced his death from "the field."

As soon as I walked in the house, I knew the man was dead; decomp has a distinct smell if you're accustomed to it. The firemen and policemen were in an intense huddle.

I banged my cot through the door. "Pronounce yet?" I asked the group.

My friend broke off to tell me the news. "We haven't been able to get the door open, even with four of us throwing our weight against it."

"Can't you take it off the hinges?" I asked.

"Hinge pins are mounted on the inside of the bathroom. And, of course, there's no bathroom window."

"Great. So now what?" That's when I found out what the huddle had been about.

The firemen were in favor of cutting the door open with a chainsaw, but the police officers were worried about the dead man accidentally getting mauled in the process. The firemen were trying to reason with the officers about their skill level, but the officers were having none of it. I threw my two cents in and sided with the officers. I didn't feel like doing any reconstructive work, especially from a chainsaw. It went back and forth until, finally, the decision was made to break in from the outside of the house so as not to harm the dead man. The firemen liked that solution; it gave them something more substantial to break than a simple door.

The firemen went to work with sledgehammers and wrecking bars, first on the brick, then the lath, and finally the plaster and tile. They made a huge mess and a tiny hole, right above where the pre-formed ABS plastic bathtub was. They didn't want to smash the tub up and risk damaging the house too much so they refrained from making the hole any larger. *Great idea—break through an exterior wall but leave the $200 bathtub alone,* I thought.

The house sat on a raised foundation. The hole was a good five-and-a-half feet off the ground. Being the smallest person at the site and the one most accustomed to handling the dead, I was nominated by my cop friend to go through the hole. After a lot of bullying and cajoling by both the firemen and the cops, I accepted the dubious honor of being stuffed through a hole in the side of a house into a bathroom where a dead man lay.

I stripped down to my undershirt and suit pants, and then allowed them to hoist me up and stuff me through the wall. I sat on the biggest fireman's shoulders and dove through the wall while the men pushed my legs in. I ended up in a dusty heap inside the mint green bathtub, no worse for wear, and from there, it was a cakewalk. The rescue men hadn't been able to push the dead man out of the way because the bathroom was so cramped that he was between the tub and door and there was nowhere to push him. He had made the perfect door wedge.

I do a lot of different things and am exposed to a lot of unique situations in my job, but I think this one was probably the most off-the-wall.

At least it was a ranch house.

PART II

Where Art Meets Science

If I want to get my wife's hackles up, I just ask her if she needs a little help with her makeup. She has never conceded my superior skills, but I point out that I have to be able to do both men and women, whereas she is a one-trick pony, so to speak. You'll see a fantastic example of this type of situation in "Men and Makeup," which relates the story of a male funeral director doing a (live) woman's makeup under "interesting" circumstances.

On a more serious note, when people hear the term "makeup" in conjunction with the dead, they immediately think of Bozo the Clown. But the real trick to applying makeup to the dead is to make it appear as if it isn't there (unless the woman was noticeably fond of makeup). That being said, there is a learning curve, and in my zeal I may have accidentally painted on people what looked like those children's candy wax lips.

Makeup, body positioning, and arranging the clothes just so are all artistic aspects of the undertaker's job with the end goal of cre-

ating a perfect memory portrait of the deceased. I think the term "mortuary science" is kind of misleading; it's certainly a science, but it's just as much an art—especially when embalming a body.

Embalming is the cornerstone of our business. The act of seeing a loved one dead is an important first step in the grieving process. Whereas a scientist follows strict protocol when performing an assay, an artist does the opposite, using whatever means necessary to achieve his vision. When preparing a body, the embalmer must be part scientist, part artist. My uncle likes to say, "Anyone can hit the fastball, but the true test is in that curveball." Though a cliché, it's very pertinent to the preparation room because you never know what you're going to be up against.

The first story in this section is certainly a "curveball," but not because of the preparation. The fireworks didn't start until well after the body was embalmed, and the brother of the dead man came in to view the body. I think the problem was that he embalmed him too well; you can judge for yourself in "The Man Who Cheated Death."

This section is a behind-the-scenes look at how we go about creating a suitable "memory portrait" (through embalming, dressing, casketing, and cosmetizing) of the decedent for the family. So come, join us for a little art, science... and makeup.

CHAPTER 13

The Man Who Cheated Death

Contributed by a member of the Sunday Martini Club

I remember well the first body I embalmed solo, but maybe for different reasons than other embalmers remember their firsts. I followed this particular call from the removal to the burial, and it was my first experience outside the classroom as a "real" bona fide undertaker.

The mortuary received the death call sometime in the early afternoon and I went with a colleague to the man's house to make the removal. He died in a hospital bed set up in the living room. It had been a slow death; I could tell by the lines of pain frozen into the features of his face and the lines of worry etched into his widow's face. The terminal illness had left a man dead and a woman not quite alive.

I offered my condolences. The widow wept. My co-worker and I did our jobs.

When we got back to the mortuary, my colleague had a bereaved family of his own coming in to make funeral arrangements and left me to my own devices. "You going to be all right?" he asked me.

"Sure," I replied. "I know what I'm doing."

He looked at me with concern. "You ever done one by your-self?" The man was a seasoned embalmer, and generally a nice person. The implication in his voice was: *This could be a diffi-cult case.*

I sidestepped the question. "I'll be fine. I promise. And if I need help I'll just wait until you're done with your arrangements."

He nodded, seemed satisfied, and went to meet with his fam-ily. I had just recently gotten my license and had only started working for the firm two weeks prior. I had been closely mon-itored and trained during my first two weeks, but on this day we happened to be especially busy, so there was nobody to help me in the preparation room. This was to be my first solo embalm-ing trip.

Death hadn't spared this poor soul's dignity—as it never seems to. "Death be not proud," I muttered the line from Donne as I undressed the man on the embalming table, "though some have called thee—." I had been a literature major at East Carolina, and after a brief, failed stint in the publishing industry, I had left dis-illusioned and broken. In the words of Wordsworth, I took a les-son from the dog and returned to what I knew; what I had grown up with—undertaking.

I washed the gentleman down and proceeded to embalm what was left of his earthly remains. Sometimes an illness can really destroy human tissues, leaving them difficult to embalm, but not with this gentleman. He took the embalming solution as though he had the vascular system of a man in his twenties. For my first solo job I was duly impressed with myself. His tissues were firm; he had good skin color and his facial features looked peaceful. Success. That night, I went home and made myself my favorite, an extra dry Kettel One martini with three blue-cheese-stuffed olives to celebrate my first solo embalming.

I made arrangements with the widow the next day. Together, we got all the details of the service set and then she proceeded to pour her heart out to me across the desk. Her husband had done everything for her. She was utterly lost without him. They hadn't been able to bear children and he was all she had in this life. I felt for the woman; I really did, and I did my best to comfort her.

On the morning of the viewing, I dressed the gentleman in a three-piece navy blue chalk stripe suit, white french cuff shirt with gold engraved cuff links, and an Italian silk gold patterned tie. I laid him out in his solid-walnut, half-couch casket and arranged him so he looked comfortable in the plush champagne-colored velvet interior. I wheeled the casket up under the torchiere lights and applied his makeup, combed his hair, put his glasses on, and placed his rosary in his hands. I stepped back, and I remember thinking to myself, *not too shabby for my first.*

I set up the flowers around the casket and arranged the family photos so that visiting friends could mosey around the parlor and look at them as though they were in the man's own living room. I polished his alto sax and placed it on its stand near the head end of the casket. After that, I filled in a guest book, printed up service brochures and memorial book marks, and lit a personalized vigil candle.

The wife was coming in to spend some private time with her husband before the viewing began. As the time drew closer I set out a fresh pitcher of water, put the dead man's favorite CD on at just the right volume, and checked and re-checked all my handiwork. Everything was perfect. I headed back into the office for my tie and jacket before I met the widow. As I bustled out of the office into the lobby, there was the widow with...the dead man!

There he stood in all his glory. Three-piece navy chalk stripe suit. White shirt. Gold silk tie. Glasses. The dead man was standing in the lobby with his wife. Alive! Talking to her! I felt like I had been sucker punched.

He turned and smiled at me.

The room started to spin, and I got tunnel vision. I grabbed onto the wall as my knees buckled.

To this day I'm glad I didn't faint because the widow walked over to me and said, "Joe, I'd like you to meet Adam's twin brother, Carter. Carter, this is the young man who has been so helpful to me."

I wiped the sweat off my brow with my suit sleeve and staggered over to the deceased's brother and introduced myself. After which, I stepped back, somewhat recovered, and said, "Do you have ESP or something? Your brother is wearing the exact same thing!" I laughed nervously, still wanting to go in the parlor and check to make sure that the casket was occupied, because I was beginning to have serious doubts. This man looked *exactly* like the man I had injected with four gallons of formalin solution.

"Identical twins can just sense these things," Carter said, deadpan.

I laughed nervously again until the widow scolded, "Carter, stop it!" She elbowed him in the ribs. "They both wore matching outfits to Carter's grandson's wedding six months ago." Then she said in a conspiratorial tone to me, "They both have the same sense of humor."

With that, Carter let out a chuckle. "You should have seen the look on your face, son!" he roared. "You thought—You thought—"

I started laughing and so did Adam's wife, until we were all laughing like maniacs. After that, I knew Adam's wife would be all right. With a family like that, how could she not be?

Later that evening, after the viewing, I called my former boss's house. "Harper Mortuary," my ex-boss's wife chirped. I had worked for them in high school, earning extra money, cutting the grass, parking cars at funerals, and taking flowers to the cemetery.

"Hey Jen," I said and proceeded to tell her the whole tale.

She laughed. "It took almost five years of Dale being in the business until that happened to him, but the twin didn't wear the same thing to the viewing. Wait until I tell him! He'll love it."

When I hung up the phone, my thoughts still on Adam's widow, I said softly to no one in particular as I mixed an extra dry martini, one of my favorite Shakespearean lines: "No longer mourn for me when I'm dead—"

CHAPTER 14

The Unwitting Smuggler

Contributed by a numismatist

M y friends say that I remind them of Pigpen from *Peanuts* because I have this cloud of junk that follows me around. It leaves behind everything you can imagine: pens, papers, keys, candy wrappers, used latex gloves, and little pieces of trash, to name a few. Truthfully, I'd leave my fingers on my nightstand most mornings if they weren't attached to my hand.

I've accepted my Pigpen status because I've been that way my entire life. I honestly don't know how I kept it together long enough to get through school. I'm a mess. And I'm not embarrassed to tell you that it's almost a weekly occurrence for my live-in girl-friend to call me at work to let me know that somehow I have her car keys on my person and that I need to return home ASAP so she can leave for work. Sadly, she's always correct.

I'm like a human black hole and pitching machine rolled into one. I manage to simultaneously collect and discard things through-out the day with reckless abandon. So it wasn't out of the ordi-nary when I lost my wallet. I have probably lost my wallet dozens of times during my tenure on this earth. Seriously. Dozens. It's happened so many times I don't even get upset anymore. It's a fact of my life.

I called and cancelled my credit cards, got a new health insurance card from Human Resources, and found some new photos of my girlfriend and cats to put in my new wallet. Problem solved. What was puzzling was when a couple of months later a funeral director from Utica, New York, called to say he had my wallet. Utica is over 2300 miles from me. This was a new record for Pigpen.

After talking to the funeral director in Utica, I figured out through brilliant detective work and interviewing my fellow colleagues how my wallet managed to travel 2300 miles by itself. One of my "clients" had unwittingly smuggled it.

It was right around Valentine's Day when I initially lost my wallet. I know, because that day at the mall I first discovered it was missing when I went to pay for the little bauble I was getting my girlfriend. Earlier that afternoon I was in the back preparing a "ship out" body. A "ship out" is a body whose removal and embalming we do for a funeral home across the country, and then load up on an airplane. The funeral director on the receiving end usually coordinates the services and burial. That particular day, I was coordinating with a funeral director from...Utica.

I had Mr. Foster in his casket, dressed, and was finishing up some quick makeup before we loaded him on his US Air flight to New York when Kaylee, the apprentice, popped her head in.

"Hey, Eric. You have five bucks for Paul's 'get well' arrangement?" she asked in her usual perky manner.

Paul is a co-worker of ours who is a real health nut but had suffered a massive heart attack a couple of days before.

"Oh, yeah," I said. I snapped my gloves off and reached for my wallet. I pulled out a five spot and handed it to her. "Spend it wisely."

She laughed and winked. "Thanks, Eric."

Kaylee can't be more than twenty and is very attractive; exactly the reason the office manager sent her around to collect money. I would have given Kaylee a fifty if she had asked me for it. As

Kaylee flounced out, I put my wallet down on the pillow next to Mr. Foster's head and called after her.

"Yeah, Eric?"

She was the only person in the firm who didn't address me as Pigpen.

"I've got to meet with a family. Could you see to it that this is put on an air tray and packaged up so I can drive it to the airport later on this afternoon?"

"Sure," she said, and flashed me a winning smile.

I left to go meet with the family and promptly forgot about my wallet on the pillow next to Mr. Foster's head. Later in the evening I drove Mr. Foster up to the airport and on my way back stopped at the mall to pick up my girlfriend's Valentine's gift, or not—because I had lost my wallet.

I received the call from the funeral director in Utica in mid-April. When they went to move Mr. Foster out of storage, where he had been until the frost had thawed and he could be buried, they heard the sound of "change falling." The funeral director went digging under the pillow and came up with my wallet. Luckily, I keep paperclips, safety pins, metal shirt stays, collector's coins, and any number of other metallic objects in my wallet; some of them fell when the casket shifted. Otherwise, my wallet would have been missing until the Apocalypse (like all the other dozens I've lost).

I guess my wallet fell to the side of the pillow, and then Kaylee had some people lift the casket into the big wooden tray that protects the casket during air travel. It got jostled down between the side of the pillow and interior of the casket where it stayed on its journey from Oregon all the way to New York State. I'm just surprised it went unnoticed during the two-hour wake and funeral.

Maybe I'll get one of those wallets with the chain on it like rock 'n' roll stars have.

CHAPTER 15

Men and Makeup

Contributed by a "Proud" undertaker

P eople assume that because I'm gay I must naturally be good at makeup. That's not the case. I'm reasonably proficient at makeup because I do it everyday. Before I joined the venerable ranks of the undertaking profession I had never done makeup before, ever. Some homosexuals—we call them fems—do wear makeup, but most of us don't. In fact, unless you got to know me well, I doubt you'd even realize I'm gay. I didn't even do makeup on a live person until three years ago.

It was St. Patty's Day. Jamie, a girlfriend of mine, was hosting a pre-party and then we were heading to a local Irish watering hole called, ironically enough, McEnery's Wake, for what was, for them, the Holy Grail of the year. They were putting on some extravaganza: all you could eat and drink and ten bands for a hundred bucks, or some deal like that. I'm a pseudo-Mick, last name is Flannery; my great-grandfather came over on the boat, and all that good stuff, so de facto, it's a holiday for me.

I showed up at Jamie's house in the early afternoon, mixed up the green beer and green jungle juice, polished the bottles of Jameson and Bushmills, and set out the shot glasses. We finished setting everything up by four o'clock, and with nothing left to do, started drinking. By the time Jamie's boyfriend came home from work we were already, as the Irish would say, half sozzled.

"What? You two not even planning on making your own party?" he asked when he found us giggling like a pair of schoolgirls on the couch.

"Oh shit, I almost forgot. I have to take a shower!" Jamie exclaimed.

So wrapped up in gossiping and drinking, Jamie hadn't even gotten ready yet. Sometimes when I drink heavily a little of that limp wrist comes out, and this was one of those times. "Oh, honey," I said, checking my watch, "you have plenty of time. People aren't even coming over for another two hours. Let's have another beer and then you can go up and get fresh."

"All right," she said not too reluctantly.

I stood up and went over to the pony keg of Guinness. "Sam? You want one?"

"Hell yeah, I've been dreaming about this all day," he said.

Needless to say, one Guinness begat three and by the time the guests started arriving Jamie still hadn't gotten ready. I threw on a couple of the Dropkick Murphys' CDs and the party got cranked up. An hour into the party it looked like an Irish Pride event, there were so many decked-out queens swilling green beer and shooting whiskey. That's when I found Jamie doing a keg stand. She kicked her feet, the signal to be let down, and everyone cheered.

I pulled her aside. "Honey, why haven't you gone and gotten ready yet? We're leaving for the bar in an hour and you're still wearing your sweats!"

She looked at me with big glassy eyes. "John, good to see you!" she said as if I was just arriving. "You know, you're right." She stabbed a finger in my face and squinted. "You're always right. I need to..." She hiccupped. "Shower."

"Come on," I grabbed her arm and escorted her through her house. I knew she wasn't in any shape to do this mission solo and I had found Sam a few minutes earlier puking his innards out—the lightweight.

"Where are you taking me?" Jamie asked in a little girl voice, and then giggled, as I dragged her up the stairs. "I thought you didn't like girls."

"Oh girl, stop it. You know I'm not interested in any of that."

"You might."

"Oh stop! I'm taking you to get ready." I dragged her into her bathroom and turned the shower on. I tested the water temperature and pointed her in the direction of it. "Strip and hop in," I commanded. "I'll guard the door so you don't get disturbed." I slammed the door and could hear laughing and a couple of loud thumps. She took twenty minutes but eventually teetered out wearing a towel. I dragged her into her room. "What do you want to wear?"

"I don't care," she sang and flopped onto her bed.

I rolled my eyes. "This is why I'm gay," I muttered under my breath. "Women!" I picked out a pair of black sex pants and a dark green camise.

I turned around and said, "How about these?"

Jamie was sound asleep.

I shook her some and she came around, clearly confused. "What's going on?" she asked.

"You need to get ready. There's a party at your house and we're leaving to go out," I explained as I put the clothes in her hands. "Put these on."

She slung the towel off and put on the clothes I had gotten out without bothering with underwear. I steered her to the bathroom. "Do your hair or whatever and then we'll leave," I said. She seemed to understand and started rummaging around in her drawers. I went downstairs to help myself to a well-deserved beer and was talking to a really cute guy when Jamie stumbled downstairs crying.

"What's wrong?" I asked her. Her mood had gone from happy drunk to crying drunk. Not a good sign.

Makeup was smeared all over her face. "I can't go out!" she wailed. "I can't do it." She pointed to her face. She looked like a bad abstract painting.

I didn't want to make her feel worse so I didn't laugh. "Just leave it," I said. "It's fine."

"No!" she wailed.

I could tell there was no use arguing with her; she wasn't leaving the house unless her makeup was done. I had a sudden flash of inspiration. "Hey girl, go lay down on the couch."

"Huh?" she said. She gave me a dumb look.

"Lay down on the couch. I'll do it for you. I'm qualified."

She complied.

"Sue," I said to one of our friends, "run up and grab her grip—er, I mean, makeup kit."

Sue returned with the makeup kit. "Hey, look!" she called. "The gay undertaker is going to give us a makeup demonstration!"

All the drinking games suddenly weren't as entertaining as a gay funeral director applying makeup to a drunken girl laid out on her couch. "I'm Shipping Up to Boston" blared from the stereo as the crowd gathered.

"Close your eyes and lie as still as possible," I told Jamie. I knelt down and from the hooting and cheering around me, you would have thought a cockfight was going on in the middle of the circle.

I'll admit, I was trashed, and it wasn't my best work by a long shot. But it was good enough to appease Jamie, and it gave the crowd a good show, as I provided running commentary and took much longer than I should have because I was hamming it up. I think she was too drunk to realize she looked like the Joker from Batman, but for my first attempt on a live person I'd give myself a "D+" grade. Hey, that's passing!

Three years later, people who were at that party, or have heard about it, still kid me about doing their makeup. Sure, I tell them, but with one stipulation, they have to lie down and close their eyes.

CHAPTER 16

A Solution for Sagging

Contributed by an Atlanta Falcons fan

W hen somebody dies, gravity pulls everything down. *Everything*. For example, take blood. Since the vascular system is no longer circulating blood, the erythrocytes (red blood cells) get pulled to the lowest point, making those areas of skin dark red. The pooling of blood in those low areas is called livor mortis. Gravity pulls other things down. Most notably on women, their breasts.

If the breasts are allowed to lie as they will, they will invariably fall to the sides. If you don't compensate for this gravitational phenomenon, women look unnatural when they are laid out for the wake. The average layman probably wouldn't be able to pinpoint exactly what wasn't right, but would just know *something* didn't look right. That something would be the lack of a bust.

I have talked to embalmers who embalm women in their bras, but I have found that to be wholly un-practical. The bra can get stained with blood if one isn't careful, and it always has to be dried out after the washing of the body, and sometimes you just can't get a bra in enough time before the embalming has to occur. So I have to come up with a way to hold the breasts up during embalming. It's the perfect solution, or so I told my aunts one afternoon.

My aunts Millie and Vicki are my dead maternal grandmother's only siblings. They live together in a big old plantation-style house on a shady, tree-lined street in your typical southern town. Since I work close to them, I try to sneak away from the mortuary at least once a week during the warm months to join the two old fire-crackers for afternoon tea on their front porch. They drink iced tea on their front porch every afternoon starting at about three o'clock and going until suppertime. As the afternoon wears on they begin pouring a little Southern Comfort in their tea. They get a little sassier with each passing hour; if you happen upon them near dark, it's damn near like being at the Friar's Club.

On this particular day I arrived late and they were giggling like schoolgirls, a sure sign of the So-Co.

"Trey, Trey," my Aunt Vicki waved to me as I crossed the lawn, "we were just talking about you."

I kissed them both and sat down in a rocking chair.

"Tea?" Aunt Millie asked.

"Please."

"The special blend?" she asked innocently.

"No thanks, Auntie. I have to get back to work."

Aunt Millie opened a silver ice bucket and used a pair of dainty tongs to drop three ice cubes into a glass. She carefully poured from a pitcher sitting on the table between her and her sister.

"Mint?"

"Please," I said.

She dropped a mint leaf into the glass and half a lemon slice.

"Sure I can't interest you in a little additive?"

"Maybe next week. Too much work."

"How dreadful. On a beautiful day like this too!" Aunt Vicki said.

"So what were you two up to?" I inquired, taking the highball glass. The three measly ice cubes looked pitiful in the giant glass.

I tasted the tea. It was watery. I knew my aunts reused tea bags—a vestige of the Depression.

"Well, Millie and I were just talking, Trey," Aunt Vicki said. "We went to Mrs. Wilbur's wake the night before last and were wondering how you..." She giggled, placing her hand over her mouth. "Shall I say un-sag certain things?" She took a sip of tea, her composure one of an innocent southern lady, but her tone suggested otherwise.

I shook my head. "You two. Always discussing the most unladylike things."

Aunt Millie looked horrified. "Us? Why never!"

I raised my eyebrow and took another swallow of tea. On top of being insipid, it was too sweet.

"We, young man, are the epitome of Southern Manners," Aunt Millie said, emphasizing her accent.

Aunt Vicki leaned in and winked. "So let us have it, Trey. What's the secret? Because old lady Wilbur was certainly saggy in life."

"It's a secret. I can't tell you."

"Come, Trey. Out with it. We won't tell a soul." Aunt Vicki crossed herself to prove her point. I guess the booze must've been affecting her because the crossing was more like a circular motion.

"Okay then. Since you both promise not to tell." I put my glass down on the table and leaned in in a conspiratorial manner. They leaned in too. I looked around dramatically and simply said, "Duct tape."

Aunt Vicki whooped with laughter and covered her mouth and nearly yelled, "Duct tape! Oh, mercy in heaven! Old lady Wilbur would be turning in her grave if she knew!"

"Quiet, you," I said. "I have Scotch tape, too."

"What ever do you mean by that, Trey?" Aunt Vicki asked. She snorted a little and took a huge gulp of tea.

I cupped my hands and approximated Pamela Anderson's bust. "Duct tape." Then I moved my hands close to my chest so that they were touching and said, "Scotch tape."

"Why, you little scamp!" Aunt Vicki yelped while Aunt Millie roared with laughter, knocking So-Co-laced tea all over her dress.

I took that as my cue. "Gotta get back to the shop. Don't forget, ladies," I yelled over my shoulder as I jogged across the yard, "don't tell my secrets!"

The Glass Eye and Other Expectations

Contributed by a Girl Scout Leader

T he chapel was full of friends and family of the diAntoni family. They were seated, patiently waiting for the service to begin. The air hung heavy with the muted sounds of a crowd trying to be quiet, but not quite being successful.

Mr. Joseph diAntoni, age 91, was laid out in the front of the chapel in blissful repose. He wore a blue chalk-stripe suit with a red silk tie, tied in a Windsor knot as Mr. diAntoni's son insisted. He had on his favorite Movado watch, and diamond cufflinks his dead wife had given him for their fifty-fifth anniversary. All in all, it was very dignified.

Mr. diAntoni's family had picked out a solid pecan casket, full couch style, meaning the entire lid of the casket was open. I had put cardboard inserts in the pant legs to give them a crisp, full appearance. Mr. diAntoni looked good for a dead man; I had even managed to tease a small smirk onto his lips during the embalming. Mr. diAntoni's family loved the way he looked. "He looks ten years younger," his granddaughter had gushed when she had seen him for the first time. They were pleased, meaning I was pleased.

I made the announcement that the casket was going to be

closed for the funeral service, and anyone not wishing to watch the closing was invited to step into the lobby. After I made the announcement, I invited the family up one last time to say their goodbyes. One by one they stepped up, stepped aside, and went back to their seats. I handed them tissues as they returned to their respective pews sniffling.

Mr. diAntoni's son, Lucas, and his wife, stepped up to the casket last. I stood at attention at the foot of the casket, ready to assist them in the covering of Mr. diAntoni with the blanket. Lucas stepped over to me and whispered, "I have some things I want to go with Dad."

"Okay," I whispered, expecting the usual: a photograph, rosary, or something of that nature.

Lucas dug into his suit pocket and held his closed hand out to me. I put my open palm under his and he released the contents of his hand into mine. I recoiled.

In my hand were Mr. diAntoni's false teeth and glass eye.

Trying not to show my discomfort at holding these items in my bare hand, I said, "We can certainly send these with your dad."

I went to tuck the items into the pocket of Mr. diAntoni's suit, but Lucas pressed up against me and whispered loudly, "Sarah, we want those where they belong."

I glanced over my shoulder at the entire chapel watching me. There were a lot of people in the audience. A lot. "Uh, Lucas," I stammered, "these teeth can't go in his mouth after he's been embalmed." Theoretically they could, but certainly not at this stage.

"Why not?" he demanded.

His wife tried shushing him, but he brushed her off.

I leaned really close to him and whispered, "The embalming process basically freezes the tissues. His jaw is frozen shut."

"What the hell is in there now?" Lucas demanded.

"A special mouth guard is in there to give him the appearance that his teeth are in."

"You got that in, why can't you put his teeth in?"

"It's too late to remove the guard and put his teeth in."

"Fine," he said nastily. "Put the teeth in his pocket. At least put the eye in."

"Lucas, I can't do that either. You should have let me know this days ago, preferably before you gave me permission to embalm him. It's simply too late now."

Lucas's voice had risen to a volume that I knew the back rows of the chapel could hear. "Why can't you put dad's eye in so he can go to his glory with it?"

My face was bright red and I was sweating. I was angry and embarrassed. Lucas was being obtuse. I didn't want to tell him the gritty details of what I had to do to prepare his father for the funeral, but he wouldn't be placated. "Look, Lucas," I snapped. "I *cannot* put his eye in."

"Then give it to me. I'll do it." His face was flushed and he had a wild look as he held his palm out to me as if he expected me to relinquish the eye. Under any other circumstances I would have gladly given him back the questionably clean prosthetic, but I was afraid of what would happen if I did.

"No," I said.

"Give it to me. Now!"

"Look, Lucas," I hissed. I dropped my tone down an octave. "Your father's eye socket is packed to make it look like he has an eye because you didn't give this to me days ago. If you want to make all these people wait twenty minutes I'd be happy to take your father in the back and see to it that his glass eye gets in. But this is something that I cannot and will not do in front of a crowd of people." I added, "And something I'm not going to let you do."

Lucas looked daggers at me. "This is the most ridiculous thing I have ever heard!" he announced.

"Do you want me to postpone the funeral a few minutes? I'd be happy to accommodate you," I reiterated.

"No, don't bother," he snapped and stormed back to his seat.

I slipped the teeth and eye into Mr. diAntoni's suit pocket, hurriedly closed the lid, turned the service over to the minister, and ran into the back to scrub my hands.

I guess the moral of my little (but very public) confrontation is that people sometimes have expectations that can't be met. These unreal expectations can also come up unexpectedly. You have to deal with them gracefully but honestly—as long as you're honest, you can't go wrong.

CHAPTER 18

Tattoo You?

Contributed by a Rolling Stones fan

T he funeral directors at my firm do the makeup on their own calls. At some funeral homes the body comes out of the preparation room as a "finished product." By that I mean the body is embalmed, dressed, casketed, and cosmetized. And at some funeral homes the women who come in and do the hairdressing also do the cosmetics. That isn't the case where I work; the decedent comes out of the morgue embalmed, dressed, and casketed. Then, the funeral directors apply the makeup under torchiere lamps in the viewing alcoves. Torchiere lamps have special colored lights in them to compliment the tone of a decedent's skin.

One day, I was doing a favor for a colleague of mine who had a doctor's appointment and had to leave early. He asked me if I would mind putting some makeup on his call, and then receive the man's daughter and let her see her father before the funeral the next day. I had nothing going on that afternoon and was happy to oblige.

I found my colleague's call to be an old, gnarled man. He was peaceful looking enough, but I could tell life had been hard on him.

His wrinkled face was a roadmap that told tales of intermittent joy, but also sorrow and hardship. His hands were tiny balls of arthritic pain, balled as if to prove he went out swinging. His family had brought in a nice dark blue polo shirt and khaki pants for him to be buried in; nothing pretentious; just practical. Practical, probably the way he had lived his life.

I began doing the makeup. It wasn't tough. He had been embalmed well and had great skin color. Unfortunately, since he was wearing short sleeves, I had to use considerable makeup to cover up the bruising on his arm. This isn't uncommon in elderly people, especially if they have been in the hospital prior to death. The intravenous needles can leave post-mortem discoloring. He had the dusky complexion of a Slavic person, and I had to use several layers of increasingly darker tan-tinted makeup before I was able to achieve a uniform color that blended well with his natural skin tone and covered the black bruises. When I was done I was pleased with how natural he looked.

The dead man's daughter arrived at the prescribed time. She had a slight accent that I couldn't place and looked very similar to her father: dark skin, hard features. I took her back into the small room we have for private viewings. Seeing her father laid out in his casket, bathed in the soft light of the torchieres, looking comfortable and peaceful, she knelt before the casket and wept.

I gave her some time. When I returned to the room she came to me and said, "Thank you for everything you've done. Dad looks better than I've seen him in ten years. He was so sick towards the end—" She bit off the end of her sentence.

Comments like that are why I do the job I do. "I'm glad you're pleased, ma'am. Is there anything I could do to enhance his appearance?" I asked.

"There is one thing—" She trailed off and then said quickly, "No, no, never mind. It's nothing."

"No, please, tell me. We'll get everything perfect."

I could tell she was hesitant, but after a second she told me, "I thought my dad had a tattoo on his arm. It was his serial number—"

"Serial number?" I was puzzled.

"Yeah, he was Hungarian. Imprisoned originally at Birkenau by the Nazis until they found out he was a Mason, then they transferred him to the Mauthausen-Gusen camps and forced him to mine granite from the infamous Wiener-Graben quarry. He was quite proud of that serial number. Almost as if he was sticking it to the Nazis by surviving their death camp and showing it to the world."

A light went off in my head, with a sudden realization. "Was it here?" I asked tracing a line on the posterior of my forearm.

"Yes!" she said.

"Oh, ma'am, I'm sorry. I thought the tattoo was bruising and covered it with makeup."

"It had gotten all stretched out and illegible in the past couple years. I just never really thought about it," she admitted.

"Here, let's let your father get sent off bearing his badge of honor," I said, taking a tissue and wiping the makeup from the once-burly arm, exposing his concentration camp serial number.

We all wear badges in one form or another, and though some fade, some tarnish, and some stretch over time, it doesn't negate their impact upon our lives. Even in death.

CHAPTER 19

Ever Seen a Dead Man Move?

Contributed by a sun worshiper/beach bum

I 've been asked more than once if I ever get scared.

"Scared of what?" I reply

"You know . . . dead people. Aren't you afraid they're going to get you?" the inquiring party asks.

I love that term, "get you." I guess people think a mortuary is just one big house of the living dead. I am here to tell you that it's not like the movies where the decedent, laying in the coffin, sits straight up and then proceeds to chase the damsel in distress through the castle. But yes, the dead *can* move. You heard me correctly. The dead *can* move . . . sometimes. Okay, it's pretty rare, but if the conditions are just right, a corpse can move. It's pretty eerie, even for somebody who is used to being around the dead all day and isn't superstitious.

Don't worry; the next wake you go to, grandma won't sit up and do a three-sixty number with her head. I hope.

The first time I had the crap scared out of me had nothing to do with the dead moving, but breathing—sort of. I was just a young buck, wet behind the ears and green all over. I'm pretty sure I was serving my apprenticeship, doing removals and running errands and things of that nature, or maybe I hadn't started it yet. Either way, it was late at night and I had been sent to some convalescent home on the other end of the earth to pick up a body. On the way back, I decided I needed a snack, so I wheeled the enormous station wagon into a fast food joint.

I pulled up to the talk box, listened to the staticky voice welcome me, and yelled my order. Upon being told some type of monetary amount that I couldn't make out, I assumed my order had been received and I pulled up to the next window.

It must have been cold out because I remember wearing a raincoat or topcoat and digging around in the pockets trying to find some cash. I found it and waited patiently for the red-eye crew to get my food. The wagon was an old gas-guzzling monster with a vinyl bench seat in the front and a radio that you had to tune. The reception was always terrible and I usually rode around in silence, as I did on that particular night. So there I was, in total silence, waiting patiently.

After a spell, I began to wonder if the place was still open. I hadn't caught a glimpse of anyone on the other side of the two little glass doors. Then it happened.

From the back I heard a loud rattle that I can best describe as a cross between a cough, a gag, and a gargle. I twisted around in the seat and looked at the supine figure under the quilt. The sound got louder, and it was definitely coming from the cot!

He's alive!

By a reflex my foot pressed the gas pedal and the station wagon shot forward in the drive-thru chute. Out of the corner of my eye I think I saw a puzzled counter attendant bringing my food to the window. All that person found was a cloud of blue smoke.

I'm not sure how I jockeyed that big wagon out of the lot without jumping the curb. It all happened too fast. I just knew I drove. The next thing I knew I was back at the mortuary listening to the decedent's chest like an idiot, trying to figure out if I heard a heartbeat or could see the chest rising and falling. Nothing. In a panic, I called the manager and told him what had happened. I felt like an even bigger idiot when he told me it was just escaping air rattling through the throat.

I guess they're still waiting at the drive-thru with my food.

That night was pretty eerie, but not nearly as much as the night a former classmate of mine died. His name was Jack. He and I went to high school together and were on the wrestling team. Jack contracted poliomyelitis—or polio—at the age of five. The disease crippled his legs and he was forced to use crutches for the rest of his life. As a result, his upper body was massive. When we wrestled, anyone could knock him off his feet, but down on the mat was his territory. He was as strong as a bear, constantly underestimated because he was a cripple. He had a winning varsity record.

I don't know if the childhood polio had anything to do with his failing heart, but Jack began having cardiac problems in his mid-thirties. A heart transplant did little good, and by age 41 he was on hospice care. He made me promise I would take care of him when he passed, and since I was close to his family, I gave them my private number to reach me as soon as Jack died. I wanted to handle everything personally.

Jack died and I received the call and went to the house to perform the removal. I loaded him onto the cot with some difficulty due to his muscle mass and took him back to the mortuary. Once in the preparation room, I flicked on the lights, wheeled the cot up next to the embalming table, and stepped out to get gowned up. When I stepped back into the room a few minutes later my heart flew into my mouth. The cover over the cot was rustling like the contents were trying to escape!

The same thought from twenty years before rushed through my head: *He's alive!*

I staggered back and hit the doorjamb. The bright fluorescent preparation room tunneled into a pinpoint of light, as my eyes tried to tell my brain to wake up and process what it was seeing. It took me a few seconds to get my wits about me before I rushed

over and unzipped the cover. At that point the rustling had subsided, and I realized what had happened. I had only heard about
it before, but there is a phenomenon in which the dead undergo
sudden involuntary muscle contractions called cadaveric spasms.

I told my colleagues about my momentarily terrifying experience and they decided to plan a little surprise for me. The next
time I went to do a removal from the hospital, I volunteered to
go up to the first floor to get the paperwork signed. When I returned to the basement, I found my colleague standing in the
hallway with the body already on the cot.

"Ready?" he asked.

"Sure," I said and prepared to turn heel and go.

That's when the morgue attendant threw off the cot quilt, leaped
off the cot, and screamed, "BOO!"

My heart stopped. I'm not kidding. It literally stopped for a
couple of seconds. I think I even put the back of my hand to my
forehead as women do when they're having a hot flash and did
a giant Lemaze-type exhale. While the two jackasses stood there
laughing their heads off, I had to sit down and catch my breath.

Apparently, my colleagues had all pitched in a couple of bucks
to bribe the morgue attendant. It worked. They nearly had to
wheel me out of that damn hospital that day, and I think I had
to throw my underwear away too.

Now, even with nearly thirty years under my belt, I still find
it hard to admit that I've had the crap scared out of me by corpses.
The dead won't hurt you, even if they do move a little. It's the
living you have to watch out for.

Family Matters

The question I'm constantly asked by my friends, mostly people in their mid-twenties, is, "How can you do what you do?" followed by, "Isn't it depressing?" They're incredulous that I'd even consider a profession that author/undertaker Thomas Lynch has dubbed "the dismal trade." But it's not a depressing job; in fact, it's an extremely rewarding one, being able to help the bereaved take those first steps in the healing process. Sure, some days are tough, especially the ones involving children and tragic deaths, but there are tough days at any job.

The first story in this section, "Lesson: Never Go to Bed Angry" is a good example of a tough day, but an important lesson. A friend of mine, who helps peer-edit my work, told me the first time she read it, it brought tears to her eyes, and she called her husband to tell him she loved him. On the surface the job may seem daunting and "depressing," but how bad can a day be that makes you call your loved one simply to tell them you love them?

Working around death has given me a greater appreciation for life, because everyday I have to face that final stage, while most people choose to ignore it. Our lives are finite; there are graveyards filled with immortals. So live each day to its fullest, because you never know if it's your last sunset.

This section is about planning the funeral service called, the "arrangement conference." The funeral service (or memorial service) is about honoring a life lived, and I believe it is a necessary ceremony for each and every human being. Its an acknowledgment that, "Hey, that person was unique and special in some way."

In addition to the exacting situations we encounter during the funeral arrangements conference, we encounter people who are in the grips of strong emotions. Ken and I had one funeral director submit to us the story of a customer who nearly killed him during the conference. After you read it you'll understand why I emailed this gentleman back and asked him if he receives combat pay.

In this section we also cover a couple of the more outlandish questions/requests that have come up during the arrangement conference. Not too long ago I was giving a presentation in my cousin's sixth grade class on ancient burial customs. After I had given my spiel and opened up the floor for questions a little boy raised his hand and asked me, "Do you bury people naked?" Caught off guard, I stammered a bit, and my mind raced to the story in this section—I was actually doing final edits on it at the time. I answered truthfully. "I've never seen it," I told him, "but as a matter of fact, I have heard of it being done!"

Heartrending workdays, killer customers, nude burials, yeah, it's all in a day's work.

CHAPTER 20

Lesson: Never Go to Bed Angry

Contributed by an urban spelunker

A woman came to the funeral home one day with the most heartbreaking story I have ever heard. Being a newly married man, I could empathize with what had transpired earlier in the week in Maddison's life because we were both newlyweds. Do you recall that old adage, "Never go to bed angry?" Maddison's story put a new spin on that axiom.

I'm thirty years old and have been working in this profession since my early teens. I started out washing cars and cutting the lawn for a little extra cash in high school, and the career kind of grew on me. In my spare time I spelunk; it is also known as vadding, building hacking, or draining. I've spelunked all over America and in Europe and South America, too. People ask me what an *urban* spelunker is. I tell them I explore abandoned factories, hospitals, rail stations, missile silos, and housing. I love seeing what was. The past. History.

I've been married eight months. The only real thing my wife and I have ever fought about is vadding. Granted, it's an extremely dangerous sport, but I love it. I have, however, since made some concessions in my spelunking because of Maddison. No marriage is perfect. You're going to fight, and if it's not about money then it'll be about something. In the past 244 days, or eight months, my wife and I have gone to bed a handful of times angry at each other, but after I met Maddison, I'll never go to bed angry ever again.

Maddison came to the funeral home on a Friday, numb with shock. Her husband had died suddenly.

Maddison's mother came in with her, and once I got them seated at the conference table, I poured them each a glass of water and pushed a box of tissues closer to them. Maddison ripped out three or four and dabbed at her red-rimmed eyes. Her mother looked a little worse for the wear; I imagined they had a rough night.

I introduced myself. "My name is Damian. I'm sorry about your husband, but he's in good hands. I'll take excellent care of him."

Maddison sniffed. She tried to force a smile but failed. I understood.

I wanted to get her and her mother loosened up a little to start them talking. It helps start the grieving process, and makes them feel safer with me. "So, how long were you married to," I consulted my notes, "Payton?"

Maddison blew her nose and took a tiny sip of water. "Pay and I have been married three years. We went to college together. We didn't date there. We actually never even met in college. Pay had to drop out his last year when his father died. He had to take over running the garage. It wasn't until after, when I moved back to the area, we kind of—discovered each other. Three years later he proposed."

Her mother squeezed her hand in encouragement.

"What garage?" I asked.

"European Specialists, over on Second Street."

"No kidding? My wife has an old, run-out Bimmer she takes there," I said.

Silence. Maddison half-smiled at me. I could tell the memory of the garage hurt.

I changed subjects. "Where do you work?"

"The bank. Sun Trust. I'm a loan officer…have you heard any-thing—" She choked off the end of her sentence. I knew what she was trying to say.

"I talked to the ME's office before you arrived. The investiga-tor told me off the record they suspect he died of a brain aneurysm. That kind of problem is usually very sudden. There is sometimes no warning."

Maddison burst into tears. Her mother held her, and I sat in silence studying my notes. After a minute or two she stopped. "Tues-day night we fought. We rarely fight, but when we do it's always about money. Money!" she spat and paused. I nodded for her to continue. "Pay was thinking about expanding the garage. Big proj-ect, but I wanted to start a family. We have no children, just a boxer. I told him we couldn't afford the expansion if we were going to have kids now. I was planning on staying home with the kids. Anyhow, we fought for a long time and Pay went to sleep in the spare bedroom."

She gulped down half of the water in her glass and looked at me steadily. "I let him go. Sometimes it's best that way. The next morning—that would be Wednesday morning—I slipped a note under the door saying if he wasn't mad at me anymore then that night we'd go to our favorite spot for dinner. It's this romantic Italian bistro in the city we can walk to from our townhouse. We like to go there on special occasions; it's so quaint and perfect. Pay proposed to me there."

I could tell she enjoyed that memory.

"I had a meeting that night and knew I would be real late get-ting home. The note also said—" She glanced at her mother and blushed. "It also said if we went to the restaurant then I'd give him his favorite dessert."

I figured the dessert wasn't food. Maddison's mom seemed oblivious to the connotation.

"That was our kind of way of mending fences."

I nodded.

Maddison continued, "That night on my way home I was think-ing Pay would be waiting for me as I walked through the door—all showered up, smelling of his cologne, and maybe he'd even have a bottle of red open so we could have a glass before we went out. He's sweet like that. We never stay mad at each other for very long. When I got home the house was completely dark, the spare bedroom door was still shut and our dog was sitting in front of the door like he was guarding it. I thought, *Fine, if he wants to be an asshole and let this continue, then I can too.* I took the dog out, fixed myself a Lean Cuisine, and went to bed without ever bothering to knock on Pay's door."

Maddison paused and squeezed her mother's hand. "So any-way, I get up for work—this is Thursday, yesterday—and the spare bedroom door is still shut. Pay usually got up and went to the garage pretty early, but I thought that maybe he wanted to avoid me, so I took the dog out, got ready for work, and left."

She drank the rest of her water, started to hyperventilate, but quickly got herself under control to finish her story. "When I got home and the door was shut, I started to get worried. It wasn't like him to not talk to me for two whole days! I went and knocked on the door. No answer. I decided to go in and I opened the door—" She broke down sobbing. Her mother put her arm around Maddison's shoulders and massaged them. Maddison continued, "There he was—"

I sat there stunned while Maddison wept. I had heard a lot of tales come across this table, but this one was probably one of the more heart-wrenching. The guy was my age! I shuffled my papers and avoided eye contact, giving her a minute, but she wasn't fin-ished.

"But—but next to him on the bed was the phone book...open to the restaurant section in the yellow pages!"

My head swam.

I guided them through the funeral arrangements. It would be awhile before the initial numbness wore off, maybe even until after the funeral. I told them what they needed to do, where they needed to be, and wrote down everything for them. They were going through the motions, just trying to get through each minute to greet the next and see if it brought less pain. The office air hung heavy with unrealized dreams, guilt, and the bitterest remorse I have ever witnessed.

When Maddison and her mom left, I called my wife. When she answered I told her without preamble, "I love you."

"What was that for?" she asked.

"I'll tell you all about it when I get home," I promised.

Maddison's story really put my marriage in a new perspective. I still do some easy building hacks from time to time because I love it, but I'd like to think I have my priorities in line now. And I tell my wife every night before I fall asleep, no matter how angry I am with her, that I love her because you never know when that time will be the last.

And there will be a last.

CHAPTER 21

Buried in the Nude

Contributed by a church choir member

W hen it comes to clothing, I've run the gamut as an under-taker. I've buried people in everything from military service uniforms to tee shirts and cut-off jean shorts. And I've buried people nude, or, at least partially nude. From a sociological point of view, I find it interesting to see what a family chooses to bury a loved one in, or what they choose *not* to bury them in.

I'm a funeral director in South Carolina. In my neck of the woods, as in the other 85 percent of the country, we mainly sell half-couch caskets. The term "half-couch" means that only half of the casket is open, hence only half of the interior "couch" is visible. The half-couch lid is split and the lower portion of the lid covers the decedent from the waist down. I think that's why I bury so many people—predominately men—partially nude. You know that old adage, "out of sight, out of mind"? The families' logic seems to be, if you can't see it, why bother? Most of my families come in to make arrangements with just a shirt, tie, and jacket for their loved ones to wear. No pants. No shoes. No socks. No underwear.

If that's what the family wants, that's fine with me, but I strongly believe in giving people some dignity. So, if the family doesn't bring in underwear, I'll ask permission to supply a pair. Most people agree to my suggestion. That wasn't the case with Mrs. Peterson.

Mrs. Peterson made a grand entrance into the conference room, a half-hour late, red-faced, and breathless. She hefted her considerable bulk into the chair, after pumping my hand vigorously while apologizing repeatedly for being late.

I assured her that her tardiness was not an issue and offered my condolences for her husband's death.

"He didn't take real good care of his-self," she said nonchalantly, drawing a cigarette out of a battered pack with her lips.

I looked at my worksheet. Mr. Peterson was 64. Relatively young. "At least you had many good years of marriage—"

She cupped her hands, fired her lighter, and waved dismissively at me. "Ain't no need for that, Hun," she said, interrupting. "He is dead. I knew it was coming; I ain't out of sorts."

"Okay," I replied. "Let's get started."

Mrs. Peterson was obviously a salt-of-the-earth type person. I liked her matter-of-fact attitude, although she had the tendency to be a bit abrasive. I could tell she drank too much, smoked too much, ate too much, didn't get offended by anything (especially bad language because she used an awful lot of it), and really didn't care what people thought of her.

During the course of the conference I gathered the biographical information on Mr. Peterson so I could file the death certificate; we picked out service folders, arranged for a minister, and Mrs. Peterson picked out a nice russet colored twenty-gauge steel casket half-couch. Then she unloaded a canvas bag she had brought in with her. Lynyrd Skynyrd CDs to be played at the visitation; a pack of Marlboro red cigarettes, a can of Budweiser, and a bottle of gin to go in with Mr. Peterson, along with his favorite John Deere hat and his fuzzy slippers.

Next, she pulled out a wrinkled dress shirt and a thin tie. "Mandy, lay him out in this," she told me, handing the hanger across the desk. "He never did wear a tie much, but I think he should look proper."

I took the clothes and hung them on the doorknob. They obviously hadn't seen an iron in ages. It wasn't at all uncommon for me to get no pants, so I casually asked, "Would you like me to put a pair of boxer shorts on your husband, ma'am?"

"What the hell for?" she asked.

She followed with a coughing bout that nearly dislodged a lung.

"Just to provide him with a dignified burial. So he doesn't have to meet his maker without drawers. I'd be happy to do it."

She coughed again, and this time I *know* a piece of lung came up. "Hell no! Jim preferred to be nude. He sat around without his pants on most of the time anyway. Nude. All the time, just wore an undershirt and those slippers."

I raised an eyebrow. "Okay."

"Now young lady," Mrs. Peterson said and wagged her finger at me, "I'm going to be checkin' to make sure my Jim ain't got drawers on. I swear that man never wore his pants, 'cept when he had to leave the house. He lived that way so he's going to be buried that way." She started laughing and coughing at the same time. I wasn't sure which one precipitated the other. When she got herself under control she said, "In fact, Jim often said—" She lost herself in another coughing/laughing fit. "Jim often said he wanted to be buried like that outlaw, you know, the one that said, 'I want to be buried face down so the whole world can kiss my ass.'" She looked at the ceiling as though revisiting a fond memory. "Yeah, he liked that, but I'm not going to do that. I'm just going to bury him the way he lived."

"I understand," I said. "My boyfriend is the same way."

"See," Mrs. Peterson said. "Men." She cackled. "They're all the same."

I laughed too. "I guess they are."

That was that. Mrs. Peterson and I bade our goodbyes.

I pressed Mr. Peterson's shirt and dressed him in it, as well as the tie and slippers and John Deere hat, nothing else.

Three days later I watched Mr. Peterson being lowered into the ground, clad only from the waist up. Mrs. Peterson wept something terrible.

Later that night when I told my boyfriend about Mrs. Peterson's last wish for her husband, he scratched his chin and said, "She might be on to something there, but I'd one-up him. Forget the shirt and tie, I want to be totally buck naked."

CHAPTER 22

Walk the Walk

Contributed by a dog lover

A few months ago I learned in the true sense the meaning of *undertaker*. The word for the profession historically describes the fact that the town cabinetmaker would *undertake* the responsibilities of caring for the dead. The profession grew from those humble origins and the name stuck. I'm not sure why—other professions *undertook* tasks—but it did. I didn't truly appreciate the value of an *undertaking* because today we now have the nice sanitary title of funeral director. But a few months ago I *undertook* for the first time.

It happened when I made funeral arrangements with an English woman named Abby. I'd judge Abby to be in her late forties, young to be a widow. Her husband, Greg, had worked for one of the big financial houses. They had met and fallen in love in London while he was working overseas, and when Greg had been transferred back to America she had followed. They married shortly thereafter. This was, according to Abby, "Over twenty years ago." Long enough that America was her home now—she was a citizen—but not long enough for her to become completely assimilated into American culture.

Abby looked very English: round, pleasant face framed by a

thick mane of straight brown hair she kept cropped neatly at shoulder length. She was thin, yet looked soft, and I imagine she kept her weight down by her "fag habit," as she called it. We Americans would call it a smoking addiction. Abby chain-smoked the entire time she was in my office.

Abby had a very continental attitude about Greg's death, and by that I mean she was very matter-of-fact. She told me between puffs on her Woodbine cigarettes that Greg's death hadn't been sudden. He had been chronically ill for some time. I could tell that she had come to grips with losing him a long time ago; what we were doing in my office was merely a formality. I have to admit, Abby had quite a stiff upper lip, and she sure hadn't lost her Cockney accent in the twenty years she had been in America. I spent most of our meeting trying to figure out what she was saying.

"Now Dere', I'll be expec'ing bof 'e 'earse and limo to pi' us up a' 'e 'ouse."

In my mind I had to translate what she said. It took a moment for me to sort out the jumbled syllables and insert the missing consonants before I got: "Now Derek, I'll be expecting both the hearse and limo to pick us up at the house."

"You want the hearse *and* limousine to pick you up at your house?" I asked carefully, so as not to offend her, yet puzzled by her request.

"Of course. It's normal in Britain to have the hearse and limousine pick up the immediate family at the house. My mum and dad are flying across the pond for the occasion. They were quite fond of Greg, you know."

I paused to translate and think before I replied. "I think I'll be able to make that happen for you."

"Splendid!" she said and clapped her hands together softly. "We'll also be needing a walker."

I thought she was talking about one of those gray aluminum assistance devices. "We don't have any walkers but we do have a wheelchair at the funeral home that I could bring along. Is it for one of your parents?" I spread my hands and looked at her. She lit a new cigarette with the tip of its predecessor and crushed the old one out. "Would the wheelchair be all right?"

"Oh my, Derek, you're so silly!" She waved her fresh cigarette in the air with one hand and reached across the desk and squeezed my hand with her other. "No, my parents don't need a wheel-chair; they're perfectly capable of walking on their own. You know, a walker to lead the cortege. Walker walks in front of the hearse and all."

I processed what she was saying before answering. "I'm sorry, Abby, it's just your accent. I'm having a little trouble understanding you."

She laughed, and stuck her cigarette between her lips so she could take both of my hands in hers. I noticed she was very com-fortable invading my personal space. "Greg used to tell people all the time that my finest and most frustrating feature was my ac-cent. And then he'd say"—she put a husky timbre in her voice, which made it even harder for me to understand—"'Abby, why can't you learn to talk American?' God, I'm going to miss him saying that." She cackled and let go of my hands. "And some other things I won't repeat to you."

I blushed

"I'm from Cheapside, you know, and I've found most of you Americans have trouble understanding the accent, but I can't under-stand the Americans from the southern states. Talk about talking through molasses! I can't understand them to save my life." She stabbed her cigarette in the air to accentuate her point.

"I can understand you pretty well, Abby. I'm just not sure what you mean by a walker."

"Oh, I guess you don't have them here in America then. Come to think of it," she grabbed her chin, "I've never actually seen one here in the States. A walker is the chap that walks in front of the hearse and leads the family members out of the drive of the residence toward the cemetery."

"Let me get this straight," I said. "You want me to walk in front of the hearse out of your driveway while you walk behind the hearse with your family?"

"Yes, and a couple of friends will accompany us too, I'm sure."

I had never heard of such a thing, but I acquiesced. "Okay Abby, I'll lead the hearse. I'll be your walker."

"Beautiful. Everything's set then?"

"I believe so. See you on Tuesday."

I went to shake hands. Abby wanted a hug.

What have I gotten myself into? I thought after she left. I had never heard of anything as ridiculous as picking the family up at the house with the hearse, much less walking in front of the hearse through a neighborhood, and I couldn't very well ask someone else to do my dirty work. The walker would have to be me.

Four days later I found myself walking in front of our black Cadillac hearse, leading it out of Abby's driveway and in the general direction of the cemetery. Abby, dressed head to toe in black, accompanied by her tiny British parents, and a couple of friends and neighbors trailed behind. It made for quite a somber procession. Halfway out of her neighborhood, I didn't feel so ridiculous anymore and began to think that maybe the Brits were onto something. The custom had a certain restrained dignity to it. When my little procession reached the edge of Abby's development, I hopped into the hearse and they piled into the limousine for the rest of the journey to the cemetery.

I learned something from Abby, and I learned it literally. Undertaking is more than just talking the talk.

CHAPTER 23

Death Knell of Jefferson and Adams

Contributed by a collegiate baseball player

T he second and third presidents of our fine country—authors of American democracy, visionaries, patriots, businessmen, politicians, and most of all, citizens—separated each other in death by mere hours. Thomas Jefferson died first, at his home Monticello in Charlottesville, Virginia, and then John Adams a few hours later, at his home hundreds of miles away in Quincy, Massachusetts, muttering the false words, "Thomas Jefferson survives." These two men, though fierce political rivals, were connected with each other and the utopian republic they had created on such a deep level that not only did they pass away within hours of each other, but they died on July 4, 1826—the fiftieth anniversary of our nation's split from British tyranny.

Some people think the story of Thomas Jefferson and John Adams amazing, ironic, or even fanciful, but after working as a mortician for the better part of my adult life, I have found that death works in mysterious ways. People are connected on many different levels that can defy social, economic, and political backgrounds. And after dealing with the Peal family, I found that these connections can transcend time, distance, and even space, but most of all, logic and reason.

I received a call from a convalescent home at about one o'clock in the morning notifying me Ida Peal had died. I loaded up my SUV and went and got her. On the way back to the funeral home I stopped at a café and got a cup of coffee to go, drank it, and then set to work embalming. I had barely begun when the phone in the morgue rang. It was my answering service, relaying a message from the convalescent home I had just come from. I was to call them back immediately.

What could be so pressing? Perhaps I had left my pager or glasses there, but I was puzzled as to why they wouldn't wait until a more sane time of day to call and let me know. I called them back anyway. The nurse on duty informed me that Evan Peal had died. Evan was Ida's husband.

I retraced my steps to the convalescent home and picked Evan up. I laid him out on another embalming table beside his wife and used a Y valve to split the hose coming from the embalming machine into two hoses. I injected the embalming fluid into them at the same time.

Later that day I met with Evan and Ida's grandniece. Her name was Omen. She explained to me that her now-dead mother had been a flower child of the '60's, hence the unusual name. I took down the biographical information Omen provided. The details chilled me.

Ida and Evan had been married sixty-seven years. They had married in '37, both at the age of 21 on June 21st. I blinked twice and checked my calendar. *Today* was the 21st of June. I called my secretary to confirm Ida's date of death because she had died right around midnight. Sure enough, she had died at 12:06 in the morning. I asked Omen for their birthdays. Their birth *dates* were both the same, but one month apart—Ida being the elder Taurus of the pair.

When Omen left I was mulling over the husband and wife who had been married for sixty-seven years and separated each other in death by only about three hours. In my tenure as an undertaker

I have seen a lot of strange things, but this really took the grand prize. Frankly, it kind of bothered me. My visit to Monticello when I was a boy popped into my head. I vaguely remembered that Thomas Jefferson had died on the same day as someone else. I hopped on the Internet and found that other person had been John Adams and that they had died on the fiftieth anniversary of our nation's independence. It made me feel a little better to realize that other people had that deep connection, too.

I read on, wanting to learn more, and eventually stopped at the epitaph on Thomas Jefferson's tombstone. His year of birth was followed by the letters "O.S."

O.S.?

It only took me a minute more to find out that the letters stood for "old style." His birth had been recorded under the old British-used Julian calendar before the Gregorian calendar became widely used in 1752, and thus, we Americans used the Julian calendar until the British stopped. I was curious about the difference between the calendars and dug a little deeper. Apparently, the conversion rate from Julian to Gregorian is the addition of eleven days for when Thomas Jefferson was born; we would know him to be born on April 13, 1743. For the years 1900-2100, the conversion is the addition of thirteen days. I did the math figuring my, my wife's, and my daughter's birthdays by the Julian calendar. I figured a couple more dates and then added thirteen days to the Peals' marriage/death date. I was floored. If their death date had been Julian and was being converted to Gregorian by the addition of thirteen days, they would have died on the 4th of July, the same day as Jefferson and Adams.

I told Omen about my findings three days later at the dual wake and she replied, "I'm not surprised. My mother, God bless her soul, was a transcendental. She smoked a little too much reefer, and dropped a bit too much acid, but she always told me things in this universe are all interconnected. I mean, look, I'm 37 years old now, and 1937 was the year my great-aunt and uncle were married. My mother told me my Aunt Ida's name was Sanskrit in origin and Ida means "insight." That is why she named me Omen. Apparently she had a premonition." She laughed.

I chuckled too, but uneasily.

As I watched the Peals' caskets being lowered on top of each other, I wanted to think it all coincidence, but the words of John Adams I had found on the Internet echoed in the back of my mind: "Facts are stubborn things; and whatever may be our wishes, our inclinations, or the dictates of our passions, they cannot alter the state of facts and evidence."

The evidence to me is that death is *not* random. Death is the product of an underlying energy that transcends countries, ethnicities, men and women, and even the human race. For whom will death's knell toll next?

CHAPTER 24

The Killer Customer

Contributed by a scratch golfer

P eople love to tell me, "It must be nice. Your clients never complain." Then they smile, wink, and nod at me, proud of their little joke. I don't argue with them, but there couldn't be a statement farther from the truth. The business is *all* customer relations and rapport. True, the dead don't complain, but their families sure can.

I deal with people at their most vulnerable and emotionally volatile. People deal with grief in many different ways. Some deal with it with grace and others...don't. The one thing I've learned in a trial-by-fire way is that an undertaker has to know how to handle difficult people. Most of them are just pushy and rude, but what about a customer who goes beyond? I had one who I honestly thought was going to kill me.

When the man showed up at my office, I knew immediately things weren't going to go smoothly. He arrived nearly an hour late, reeking of booze, and didn't bother taking his sunglasses off as he stalked into the office, sitting down opposite me at the conference table, leaving me standing, hand extended. I slowly withdrew my hand and sat down. I gave a slow nod at the man, who sat in his chair and stared at me behind his shades with an arrogant expression. I took note of the black leather vest with a riding club logo emblazoned on it.

I introduced myself and he gave me a one-word answer for his name. I doubt it was his real name unless his mother named him after something in the reptile family. "Okay," I replied, and made a note.

We sat in silence and stared at each other before he decided to break the silence with a well-rehearsed, poetic verse. "This is some fucked up shit, man," he said.

I raised my eyebrows and took the bait. "What is?"

"My old lady dyin' is what."

He reclined back in his chair, and folded his massive tattoo-covered arms.

"Well, Snake," I checked my worksheet, "your mother was 83. Looks like she had a nice full life."

He ignored me. "You know I just couldn't go see her in that place," he said, referring to the nursing home she was in. "Place stank like piss and all those old people, near death, just sitting around in their chairs waitin' to die. I couldn't see Ma there. Haven't seen her in six or seven years."

He was letting me see where his hostility and resentment were bubbling up from. Clearly, he was overcome with feelings of guilt and remorse. Believe it or not, that's common in most people. They ask themselves, "Could I have visited the person or called them more?" With this particular gentleman, acute guilt coupled with the fact that he was a bear of a person and had an aggressive personality.

I had to play it cool.

I got him talking, calmed his feelings, and made some progress in the arrangements. We were about halfway through when Snake became agitated.

He stood up so suddenly that his chair crashed over. "I want to see Ma now!" he yelled, poking a meaty finger into the burled walnut conference table. I stared at the sunglasses covering his eyes, trying to appear cool though my heart was racing. The room was silent except for the chain at his waist clinking against the table.

"Your mother is in the preparation room. You can't see her right now," I said. "Maybe later."

I moved my writing hand under the table so Snake couldn't see it was shaking.

He leaned all the way across the table and put his finger right in my face. I could see the veins bulging out of his forearms. "Maybe you didn't hear me correctly, Junior."

Junior? Oh shit, I'm going to die!

His whiskey-scented breath washed over my face. "I haven't seen Ma in eight years. I'm seeing her now!" He made a fist and pounded it on the table to accentuate his point. The table shook.

I only weigh a hundred and fifty pounds soaking wet and have the physique of an infant, but I remained seated and spoke to Snake in the most authoritative tone I could muster. "Snake," I said firmly, "you need to sit down right now. I told you, your mother is being prepared and you can't see her until later. And if you continue to act this way this conference is over." I closed my notebook, clicked my pen, and stared at him with a questioning look on my face. "What will it be?"

Snake's finger was back in my face and it inched closer. Each finger was about the size of a hotdog and his nails were bitten to the quick. I thought for sure my windpipe was about to get crushed by his toilet-seat-size hands, but I continued to stare at him. My heart was in my throat and I couldn't swallow. I eased my hand to the right where the telephone was sitting. I figured I could at least dial the "9" and one of the "1's" before he ripped my head from my body. The meaty finger retreated and he quietly picked his seat up and lowered himself into it.

"Shall we continue?" I asked as if I were asking what the weather was like.

He nodded and hung his head.

I opened my notebook and clicked my pen. "So, where did we leave off?"

Five minutes later his shades were off. Ten minutes after that, he cracked a joke. On his way out he shook my hand and apologized for "being such a jerk," and re-introduced himself as Dean. He offered his hand and I shook it.

Sometimes I need to pat an old lady's hand and cry with her, and other times I need to stare down a 275-pound biker. The job is unpredictable like that, but the fact remains that I need to know how to handle difficult situations and difficult people. And, believe me, there is no shortage of difficult people.

CHAPTER 25

The Comedian

Contributed by an open-mic night comedian

I have been a comedian my entire life. Funeral directing was my backup plan, still is, but until my comedy act can start paying the bills, I have to go out on night calls. It's one thing to be up in the middle of the night hauling one of the dearly departed from bed, and an entirely different thing to be up at that same time of night in a smoky dive, clutching a whiskey-smelling microphone in front of a tough crowd. The latter gets my juices flowing a lot more than the former.

Death isn't a laughing matter. But laughter does help the healing process. That's my philosophy.

An older woman who showed up at my mortuary awhile back is still firmly planted in my memory—partly because she appeared in my life the same day I scored my first paying comedy gig (a hundred smackeroos) and mostly because she is not the type that one forgets. The woman had the innate toughness of someone who has lived a long time in a short number of years—you could see it in her face. Nary a tear was shed as she looked me straight in the eye and shook my hand firmly. She had come to see me because her only daughter was dead.

I ushered Mrs. Smith into my office. She walked with the slightest of limps, hardly using the cane she carried. Her gray hair was wound into a tight bun and perched upon the top of her head like a bird's nest in danger of falling off. She hefted her plump rear end into one of the chairs facing my desk, folded her hands on the top of my faux-mahogany desk, and began to talk.

Mrs. Smith's daughter was only 40 years old. She had died due to complications of diabetes. She was the only child, and Mrs. Smith's husband had died a number of years ago. That much she told me. She didn't fill me in on the when, where, or how. She had relatives in Florida, where she was going to be moving as soon as she buried her daughter.

It had been a long, hard, trying road and she was glad it was over. Apparently, toward the end things had gotten pretty bad. "I used to look like Jane Fonda before my daughter got sick," Mrs. Smith said. "Now look at me!" She laughed sharply and sat back in her chair, pleased with her joke. I had yet to speak, but knew we were going to get along fine.

"Mrs. Smith, can I get you a refreshment? Coffee, tea, mineral water, soda...Manhattan?"

"Finally! A man after my own heart! Knob Creek, three cubes, no peel," she rasped.

"Would you like that shaken or stirred, Mrs. Bond?"

She cackled. "I don't care as long as it has lots of booze in it!"

"The only kind I know how to make."

Her stony façade cracked and the floodgates opened. Mrs. Smith started regaling me with stories about her youth, when she and her husband had been an acrobatics team for the circus. "How I got this damned limp!" she exclaimed, pointing into the air and then tapping her bum leg. Then she proceeded to tell me the story of the nasty fall that had ended her career and nearly killed her husband. It was a long drawn-out saga that ended with, "I wanted to stay with the circus and the only thing I could do was become the bearded lady. That's when my husband developed an affection for the sauce." She leaned over the desk, pointing her cigarette at me, and whispered conspiratorially, "Me too! But it hasn't killed me, only pickled me."

The tales went on and on. Tales about her daughter, family trips, and her career teaching gymnastics with a bum leg at her studio. I laughed along with her, all the while performing my job of taking notes and gathering information for the funeral service.

Mrs. Smith seemed to delight in throwing out cheesy one-liners about the death profession. such as "You're the last person to let someone down!" and "I bet people are just dying to get in here!" Then she would give her sharp, biting laugh that ended in a coughing fit from a lifetime of chain smoking, a habit she continued while in my office. My ashtray overflowed with lipstick-printed slim cigarettes.

While we were making arrangements, she kept saying "There's something I want to tell you that I can't remember." Then she would get sidetracked on her life's story. By the end of all her stories I had managed to get all the funeral details hammered out.

Once again she said to me, "There's something I want to tell you that I can't remember."

"That's all right," I told her. "I'll go over the price agreement with you and if you remember later, you can call me."

I discussed all the itemized charges on the price agreement and had gotten to the total when she burst out, "I know what I wanted to tell you!"

I raised my eyebrows.

She leaned over the desk and whispered clandestinely to me as if there were other people who might overhear, "She doesn't have any legs."

Without missing a beat I stared back at her and whispered, "Same price."

She sat back and laughed so hard tears came to her eyes. She started coughing and slapping her leg and I couldn't tell where the coughing began and the laughter ended. I waited patiently with a big stupid grin on my face.

After Mrs. Smith composed herself and I was walking her out of the funeral home, she shook my hand and said soberly, "Thank you, Mr. Joke. You have made this so easy. I was really dreading coming in and doing this even though my daughter—" her voice cracked, "is in a much better place. I haven't laughed this hard in ages. I really needed it. To be frank with you, I'm dreading moving to Florida. My cousins are all a bunch of stuffed shirts."

"Mrs. Smith, if you ever want to laugh just call me and it would be my pleasure." And I meant it. "As for your family in Florida, maybe they need a little humor in their lives. Something you can certainly offer them."

CHAPTER 26

Hearse of a Different Make

Contributed by a Eucharistic minister

T ransporting the dead is a big part of my job. In our frag-
mented society, it's not at all uncommon for someone to
die hundreds of miles from the family plot. How do we
get them to where they need to go? In the old days, the rail-
roads were used. But today, if human remains need to be transported, it's done via hearse if the distance isn't too great, or more
frequently, via airliner. Believe it or not, the last time you boarded
a flight to Las Vegas to do some gambling, or California for a
romantic weekend in Napa, or Florida to soak up the sunshine,
you were more than likely traveling with a dead passenger in the
cargo hold. It's standard fare, although there are less conven-
tional methods.

I once served a family who wanted to take "Dad" back to his
final resting place themselves. And by that I mean in the back
of a battered Dodge pickup truck. I really don't think it was a
matter of money, but rather a promise made. What could I do?
I honored their request. These folks backed their pickup into the
garage. We hefted the twenty-gauge steel casket into the bed,
covered it with a quilt, and strapped it into place. I gave them

the burial/transport permit and stood in the parking lot waving good-bye as they headed for a family plot in the Black Hills of North Dakota.

It's not illegal to do something like that, though most people are uncomfortable transporting a dead loved one propped in the back seat or lying in the bed of a truck. It conjures up images of *National Lampoon's Vacation* in my mind, and I'm sure in the minds of most other people. The typical family would prefer to let the funeral home take care of the livery services. But when I loaded "Dad" into that pickup truck and waved good-bye, I didn't think in a million years a similar saga would unfold in reverse.

Several years later a family walked through my front door and told me their mother was dead. I offered them my sincerest condolences and ushered the two sons and daughter of the dead woman into my office. I served them coffee and fresh muffins and we sat and talked about the funeral service. I collected as much biographical information about the dead woman as they could remember—information I needed to complete the death certificate and file it with the state. Then I got around to the biggie: where is "Mom"?

The son offhandedly told me, "Around back."

I was caught off guard and replied, "Huh?" With a dim-witted look.

The son took the last bite of his third muffin and reiterated, "Around back." Then he added, "In the pickup."

I guess I gave them a horrified look because the daughter quickly chimed in, "We brought her here in the truck. Thought we'd save you a trip."

"Save me a trip?" I know I was repeating her, but it was all I could think of to say.

"Well, sure," the son said, grabbing a fourth muffin. "She died. I picked her up an' laid her in the back of my pickup an' came on over here."

I hopped up and practically ran outside, the three clients trailing behind me. The pickup was in one of our many parking spaces just like any other car visiting the establishment. I peered inside the truck bed and sure enough, a figure lay there swaddled in white sheets.

Hello, Mom.

CHAPTER 27

Shot-Putted Urn

Contributed by a muscle car restorer

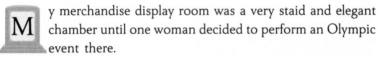y merchandise display room was a very staid and elegant chamber until one woman decided to perform an Olympic event there.

I've worked very hard changing and tweaking things over the years to ensure that the display room isn't too intimidating to my customers, yet conveys the message that their loved ones are going to get the finest products. I've found there's no good way to display visual reminders of their loved ones' deaths, but the impact of coming face to face with caskets, urns, and burial vaults can be minimized, and I've tried to present my merchandise in the least threatening way possible.

My display room is an L-shaped area with the urns, models of the burial vaults, and memorial jewelry visible as you first enter, and the casket display once you turn the corner. A bubbling fountain flanked by plush couches and potted plants softens the room, and, of course, I have classical music piped in.

The day I met the shot-putter, I had an appointment with a woman and her brother. Their father had died and his wish was to be cremated and then have a memorial mass at one of the local Catholic churches—after which, half of him was to be buried in the diocesan cemetery and the other half scattered in the ocean. Their father had been in the Navy during the Second World War, and he wanted to be with his wife (who already was in the cemetery) as well as his mistress, the sea. Fine, that's the beauty of cremation; many wishes can be fulfilled regarding the remains, while with a traditional burial, the person can only be interred in one place.

In talking to the mourners in my office, I learned their father had been something of a Renaissance man. Not only had he been a rough-and-tumble sailor, but he had enjoyed building ship models, taught himself to play the piano, and in his later years, took gourmet cooking classes at the local community college. Before we went into the selection room, his daughter told me, "I think we should put Dad in something that will fit his personality: masculine, yet artistic, and blue... for the sea."

I had just the thing for her.

I took the woman and her brother into the display room to a cerulean colored cloisonné urn that sat on a shelf where the two lengths of the L-shaped room come together. I thought it was perfect for what she was describing—masculine, and yet artistic. I picked it up and handed it to the woman.

She hefted the urn, as if to weigh it. "Okay, okay," as she turned the multi-colored enameled container around in her hands. "May I open it?"

"Go ahead," I replied.

She twisted the lid off, peeked inside, screamed, and hurled the urn down the length of the casket display area with a prowess that would have made a shot-putter at a track meet take notice.

The urn ricocheted off a sixteen-gauge steel casket at the far end of the room with a loud *bing* and then partially shattered when it hit the tile floor. A small furry form shot out of the wreckage and disappeared behind a casket. The woman's brother cringed, and the woman stood there in horror as if she couldn't believe what she had just done.

I'm pretty unflappable, so I turned to the woman, and said, "What? Wrong color?"

She gave a short laugh, as if she didn't hear me. "Oh my—"

I cut her off. "Mouse? They tore down that old church next door a month ago and apparently it disturbed their nest. We've been having a mouse problem here for a couple of weeks. Somehow, that little guy managed to get *into* the urn. Weird. I'm really sorry to scare you like that."

"It's not your fault," she protested.

"Nice toss though."

"Thanks, I mean—"

"We'll pay for it," the brother chimed in.

"No. No. Don't worry about it," I said, waving my hand in a dismissive way. I didn't want this family going around saying I had a mouse problem. "It's no big deal. We'll pick something else out. Something without a surprise hiding in it."

"No, no," the woman said, dazed. "That one was perfect. That was Dad."

"You sure?" I asked.

"I'm sure."

I ordered a replacement urn for their father and called the exterminator back. I thought he was going to have a seizure, he was laughing so hard when I replayed what had happened, acting out the motions in the display room and everything. Apparently a mouse in an urn was a first, even for his line of business, and he's probably seen mice in all sorts of places. He thinks the mouse must have crawled into the urn when the lid was ajar and it closed behind him; he just got lucky we picked it up before he died in there.

I still have the partially shattered urn sitting on a shelf in my office. When people ask me why it's there, I tell them about the day I had an Olympic shot-putter in my showroom.

CHAPTER 28

Last Wishes

Contributed by a website designer

I met Claire Morgan, a woman who had founded a local hospice program, through a friend of mine. Claire was a former nurse who had lost her husband to a terminal illness at a young age. She was left with enough money that she didn't have to work another day in her life. Instead of taking her money and moving to the Sun Belt as most people would have done, Claire decided to do something to help families going through the same thing she had gone through.

Relatively speaking, it was a small hospice—ten nurses and just under one hundred patients. Claire wanted to keep it small to maximize patient care and minimize stress on the families of the dying. It worked. Word quickly spread about this wonderful new facility, and Claire had to hire more nurses to keep the same patient/nurse ratio.

The first time I met Claire Morgan was at a Christmas party our mutual friend was hosting. She had never come before because she and her husband had always gone to his boss's Christmas Eve party.

"My husband recently died," Claire said to me, "and I just can't stand the thought of going to a cocktail party and doing nothing but accepting half-hearted sympathies from his colleagues. The idea is simply macabre. I just wanted to...come somewhere slightly anonymous and soak up holiday cheer."

I agreed. As we talked more, she told me of her plans to form a hospice organization. I encouraged her, telling her what she planned to do would provide an important step in the dying process, and that I, as one of the town's many funeral directors, saw the importance of hospice work on a daily basis. She thanked me for my kind words and I didn't see her until the next Christmas party.

I asked her how her hospice program was coming. She looked surprised that I had remembered, but then told me she had just opened her doors for business the month before. She had named her company Stone Hospice after her late husband, Stone Morgan. I congratulated her and reiterated my previous year's praises of the work hospices do.

A couple of weeks later, Claire called my office and asked me if I'd be available to make some arrangements with one of her patients. I told her I'd be delighted. I met with Claire, the patient, and the patient's daughter. The patient died a few weeks later and I buried him.

Over the following years I received periodic calls from Claire to make arrangements for her patients. Some would linger. Some would die quickly. And just as she had cared for them when they were dying, I would treat them with the same dignity once they had died.

Claire and I had been working together a long time when she called me down to her office to make arrangements. It was unusual, since I usually went to the patient's house for such meetings, but I've found in my business nothing is unusual.

When I arrived I gave her a quick hug. "Where's the patient?" I asked.

"Sit down, R.J.," Claire said. "I have something to tell you."

"Oh?"

"I'm the patient. You're here to make arrangements for me."

"No!" I said. "You?"

"It's cancer. Inoperable."

"Claire—"

She held up her hand. I wasn't sure if it was my imagination, or if her cheeks didn't look as full as I remembered. "Look, R.J., we both deal with death on a daily basis. It's not something most people want to do, but it's something that has to be done. There have to be people like us in society, people who aren't afraid to look death in the face day in and day out. Sure, I'm angry that I feel like I've been cheated out of a full life, but I'm not *scared* to die."

"Radiation and chemo?" I asked.

"Already tried. Didn't work. I've got three months to live. I want you to handle things when the time comes."

Claire told me the details of the funeral she wanted, and she asked me to care for her family as she had seen me care for countless grieving families that had passed through her program. She wanted assorted cheeses and wine offered at her viewing. She wanted a harpist and her favorite Beatles song played during the service. She wanted the pallbearers to wear white gloves and yellow ribbons, and most of all, she wanted two white doves released in the cemetery, one for her and one for Stone.

When I left, we hugged.

Claire Morgan died sixty-four days later. She was 58.

She is the only person I know who had the courage to face death with such grace when her husband died, and then face her own mortality with honesty, poise, and...courage.

The hospice has since flourished. I think it is a fine legacy to a courageous woman.

PART IV

Wakes, Funerals, and Burials

I was sitting outside a funeral one day when two men pulled pistols and had a good ol' fashioned shootout before my very eyes. Surprised? I sure as hell was, but as at any social event, anything can happen at a funeral, and usually does. Sometimes the attendees' tensions boil over as seen in "Wake Combat." Other times some total, random, external force that has nothing to do with the funeral, can affect it, as in "Duel at High Noon." Either way, wild stuff can, and does, happen. I hope, though, you'll never have to attend a funeral as "exciting" as some in this section.

What exactly is a funeral?

We've all been to them, some of you readers have even arranged them, and they're never joyous occasions, so why do we even bother having them? A funeral is the ceremonial marking of someone's death. It's a rite of passage just like a baptism, wedding, or graduation, all important events. The traditional flow of the American funeral includes a wake (interchangeable with "viewing"), funeral service, and then a burial.

There is still that "traditional" template, but in 21st century America there is no standard. Families today have a lot of choices, sometimes I think too many. With the increase in popularity of cremation, not to mention the burgeoning demand for green burial, the sky is the limit for memorialization and funeralization. Whatever the wishes of the family, the funeral director's goal is to provide a personalized memorable occasion.

Unfortunately, there is a common pitfall. Many companies advertise funeral products that boast they will create a memorable service. But in fact, products will not create memories. People do. I think this point will become evident in a story like "A Hug, a Hope." Don't get me wrong, products can certainly augment a service, but a certain type of stationery can't replace the memory of a granddaughter singing a favorite song of her grandmother's during the service, or an honor guard presenting a flag for one of America's fallen heroes.

While having dinner with my parents not too long ago, I told them about my latest book—the one you're reading now. After hearing its premise, my dad demanded a "for instance." I told him about "Duel at High Noon." At the end he said, "How come this is the first time I'm hearing about this!"

"I was saving it for the book," I told him. "You're just going to have to wait and read the rest."

So, read on.

CHAPTER 29

My Bar Story

Contributed by a part-time model

W hat's the craziest thing that's ever happened to you?"
I invariably hear this after someone finds out that I'm in the funeral business. People are insatiably curious about the dead and those who work around them. Of course, I would hate to disappoint anyone, so I happily share the most outlandish, ridiculous thing that has ever happened to me in my life. It's the tale of a dead Jesuit priest and it's usually told in bars.

The funeral home I used to work for was located near a Jesuit-run high school. We had a contract with the order to provide funeral services when one of its members died.

Let me give you a little background. The Jesuits are a religious order of the Roman Catholic Church, formed in the 16th century by Saint Ignatius of Loyola. Their members can be found in over 100 countries, where they are associated with higher learning and run a number of high schools and universities.

My adventure began when one of the priests, who we'll call "Father Iggy" in honor of the founder of the order, died. Father

Iggy was an English teacher at the high school who coached a number of sports teams and was a generally upstanding guy. The students loved and respected him as a teacher, coach, and mentor, and former students routinely called upon him to perform their weddings. From what I heard, Father Iggy was also an active volunteer in the community and was recognized by the Pope himself for his service. When he died, I was assigned to handle his funeral.

I had handled several big ceremonies and was confident in my ability to handle the services for a well-known priest.

I did the removal from the rectory and embalmed Father Iggy. The following day I met with the senior priest and set the details of the funeral: an evening viewing in the church, Mass of Christian Burial the following day, and burial in the local Catholic cemetery.

On the morning of the viewing, a couple of Jesuits came over and we dressed Father Iggy in the priest's traditional black cassock. I applied the barest traces of makeup on his face to give him a little ruddiness and put him in the most economical casket available. Our "cloth covered casket," or "minimum casket," is basically fiberboard covered with black felt called doeskin. Because of their vow of poverty, priests are laid to rest in our most basic casket. The black doeskin represents the color of the Jesuit cassock.

In addition to being minimalistic, priests' caskets differ from others in that they have removable lids that allow the entire body to be seen, instead of just the upper-half, as is more typical. The design allows for two lines of people to file by during the viewing instead of just one. Priests usually have well-attended viewings and funerals.

I unscrewed the lid's hinges before placing Father Iggy in the casket. Without a hitch, I transported the deceased priest to church and laid him out in the sanctuary for the viewing. The pews were rearranged to let the two lines of people file by. That evening,

over eight hundred friends and acquaintances came to pay their
respects.

The next day, the church was packed—standing room only. The
school had the day off in observance of Father Iggy's passing.
Current students, former students, parents, members of the church,
employees of the diocese, and fellow priests choked the pews and
aisles.

At the proper time, I wheeled the now-closed casket into the
vestibule and gathered the pallbearers to give them their instruc-
tions. On the stroke of ten, the officiating priests blessed the casket and the white cloth, or the "pall," was placed. As the priests
processed up the aisle, I signaled the pallbearers to lift the casket off the small cart called the "church truck" and carry it to its
place at the front of the sanctuary. Generally we roll the casket
up the aisle on the church truck, but the senior priest wanted the
pallbearers to be more than ceremonial, so they carried it.

Everything went as planned until the casket reached the second pew from the front. A loud, ominous cracking sound ushered in an unsightly scene as the bottom of the casket fell out.
Down with it fell Father Iggy. He hit the marble floor with an
undignified thump. The crowd's collective gasp echoed through
the vaulted eaves. The pallbearers, still holding the handles of the
pall-covered casket, stood dumbstruck staring down at the floor,
where Father Iggy still clutched his ceremonial chalice.

I knew I had to take charge—fast.

I pushed the pallbearers to the front of the sanctuary and in-
structed them to lay the shell down. I shooed out the priests who
occupied the front pew and asked the pallbearers to pick up Father
Iggy and place him on the bench. The pallbearers were in such
a state of panic that they didn't hesitate.

Next I had the pallbearers create a human shield to spare the
mourners the macabre sight of the dead man lying on the front
pew. Everything happened so fast that I didn't have time to be
scared. I motioned one of my colleagues over and told him to

go back to the funeral home for a new casket as quickly as possible.

While he rushed away, I dragged the remnants of the broken casket to the rear of the church. Fortunately, the funeral home was just down the block, and the new casket arrived in minutes. With as much dignity as we could muster, the pallbearers and I placed Father Iggy into his new casket and re-draped the pall. The service proceeded without further incident, but as a precaution, meaning no disrespect to the senior priest, I had the pallbearers wheel Father Iggy out on the church truck instead of carrying him.

The most difficult thing I've ever done in my life was to walk out of that church with Father Iggy, knowing that every pair of eyes in the congregation was fixed on me—and every mind was wondering, *what kind of funeral home allows a priest to fall out of his casket?*

I later figured out what caused Father Iggy's second coming. The "minimum caskets" are held together at the joints by wooden dowels and glue. Our company policy was to order the minimum caskets in bulk to receive a discount. Father Iggy's first casket had probably been stored in the basement so long that the glue had dried out—and the joints had come apart from the weight of his body.

After the "Father Iggy Incident," as it came to be known, there was no more ordering in bulk.

CHAPTER 30

The Dove

Contributed by an amateur surfer

O ne day I killed a dove—a beautiful, innocent white dove. The symbol of innocence and purity—and I murdered it. Normally, I release them at graveside services, but not on this day. Instead of releasing the bird as a symbol of the deceased's freed soul, I unceremoniously stomped it. Now, before you start calling me a sadist or sociopath or report me to PETA, let me tell you of the events leading up to the slaying. It went something like this:

I was driving the hearse for a dead man whose funeral arrangements I had made. I was to lead the funeral procession from the funeral home, where the services had been, to the cemetery. Before we left, the wife pitched me an unusual request: Could she accompany her husband on his last ride? In some areas of the country I understand it is common practice for the deceased's spouse to ride in the hearse with the funeral director, but it is uncommon in my area.

"I'd be happy to have you accompany me and your late husband," I told the widow.

I rode in uneasy stillness with this very WASPy woman wearing her wide brimmed '40s style hat. In the stagnant, plastic-smelling car air, the silence was so thick I could almost cut it with a dull knife. Normally, I am very easygoing around the bereaved families I serve, and I had been comfortable with this widow until the moment she got into the hearse with me. But now I felt like I was fifteen all over again, learning to drive with my mother in the other seat stamping on her imaginary brake every three seconds. With every bump, every abrupt stop or acceleration, I felt her watching me, evaluating me, judging me. I was so preoccupied with driving perfectly that I nearly missed a couple of turns.

I'm sure the woman had so many emotions overwhelming her that she couldn't even function normally, but the situation was nerve-wracking for me. We were almost at our destination, when the unthinkable happened.

I pulled through the giant stone pillars of the Rest Haven Cemetery and a large dove flapped down from one of the pillars and landed right in front of the hearse. I braked hard and came to a near standstill. The beautiful bird in the road seemed not to care that a giant, smoke-belching beast was heading straight for it. I inched forward, riding the brake, and nudged the Federal Coach to the right and partially up onto the grass. Wouldn't you know that that bird walked to the right?

I slammed on the brakes and winced. I could feel the widow's disapproving glare as she watched the saga unfold in front of her. I could almost hear her inner voice shout at me: *Can't you even outwit a bird? My husband is in the back, dead!* I cranked the wheel all the way to the left and eased off the brake. Of course, to spite me, the dove walked left.

The limousine carrying the rest of the family was right behind me, so I couldn't back up. I was trapped. I made a game time decision. I decided to get out and shoo the bird away. I threw the hearse in park and got out. The bird, seemingly unconcerned by my presence, walked away from me and into the grass. *There,* I thought, *that ought to take care of him.* I hopped back into the hearse, and back into the roadway the dove walked.

That's it, I thought, *if I just move the hearse up, it'll be smart enough to fly away.* So, my foot on the brake, I steered the hearse closer and closer and closer... and I hit the bird. In the silence of the hearse the squawking of the injured dove was loud, very loud.

I winced.

The widow winced.

What could I do? I drove forward.

In the rearview mirror I watched as the bird, with a wing obviously broken, flapped about on the pavement briefly before the limousine crushed it. The widow jumped when the squawking suddenly ceased with a loud *crunch*. And I watched further as each of the thirty cars in the procession ran over the carcass.

While I'm not the one who actually killed the dove, a lawyer might say the extent of my culpability was "reckless endangerment." Regardless of the legalities of who actually *killed* the bird, I was treated to the widow's withering stare the whole time the minister committed her husband's body to the ground.

CHAPTER 31

A Hug, a Hope

Contributed by a professional speaker

I t was the middle of winter. The type of day when the grass is frozen and crunches underfoot, but the sun shines brightly and there's not a cloud to be seen. The type of day when the wind blows just enough to remind you winter is still there, but the sunshine, courting favor with the cold, reminds you spring is only around the corner. I was young, just starting my apprenticeship, standing, hands buried deep in my woolen topcoat, neck compressed into a scarf, watching the men from the vault company do their somber work.

The tent flapped in the breeze as the two men sealed the concrete vault and cranked the entire package into the yawning hole cut into the earth. The congregation had long since gone to their luncheon to laugh, reminisce, eat and maybe drink. I had chosen to stay and watch. I didn't inspect their work, but observed it like a voyeur. As the men broke down the bier, I caught the eye of a woman standing a stone's throw away at another headstone. She turned away quickly but then looked again as if she was gaining her courage.

The next time I looked, she was staring at me. It was a bla-
tant, open stare that some might call curious and some rude. But
by the look in her eyes I could tell it was neither.

I went over to where she was standing.

"Can I help you with something?" I asked, and flashed a smile.
The woman was dressed professionally, like a businesswoman on
her lunch break. She was middle-aged and pleasant looking. She
had kind, soft eyes. The wrinkles around them told a harder, different story.

"I— You look—" Her breaths gave off puffs of steam as she
spoke. "Never mind," she finished lamely.

I looked at the grave where she stood. The headstone had a
man's name on it. He had died very young, I noted. He had been
my age. "Your son?"

She bit her bottom lip and nodded. We stood in silence for a
few moments. "I miss him. I miss him so much," she simply stated.
"He was such a good kid. Our first—" She put her chin on her
chest to collect herself. "Somebody ran a red light. It was...the
middle of the day. Nobody was drunk or anything. He was just
at the wrong intersection that day."

She shook her head as if confused while staring at the headstone, and then looked at me ruefully. "I'm sorry—"

I cut her off. "Don't be."

She knelt down and traced the name engraved into the granite while talking to me. She must have gone on for five minutes
or more about how much she missed her son. I listened. When she
was done with her monologue she asked, "May I give you a hug?"

Without hesitation I answered, "Sure."

We embraced and I felt her crying softly. When she let go,
she stepped back and said, "Thank you for that. You remind me
so much of him. Kind. Polite. Well mannered. Your mother must
be so proud of you. I—I needed a hug from my son today. Thank
you for giving me that."

I never did ask her name, and she never asked mine. We parted ways and I haven't seen her since.

You can touch someone's life in a profound way every day if you just slow down and recognize the opportunity.

Give someone a hug. Give someone hope.

CHAPTER 32

Wake Combat

Contributed by a collegiate swimmer

here's something about a funeral that makes it the perfect venue for a fight. I've seen all sorts of different fights take place at my funeral home, from little verbal skirmishes to knockdown, drag-out fistfights. I've even had to hire security (at the behest of the family) to keep the peace.

Money. Lovers. Attention. The list of things that families fight about is endless, but instead of facing the problems as they come, most people choose to bottle it up and wait. The pressure builds and a death in the family can cause the pot to boil over.

The most violent fight I can remember is one that happened years ago. I can't remember the name of the family, but I remember the two sons of the dead man as vividly as I can picture my own sons. It was an Irish family. They had a McSomething type name. The two sons, Brian and James, came in to make the funeral arrangements without their mother. She was too distraught over the death of her husband to come in. The man was in his late forties and the death was entirely unexpected.

The boys were in their late twenties. I couldn't tell if they were twins or not. They looked an awful lot alike except Brian was slightly taller than James and had a large scar over his right eye.

The brothers came into my office, sat down, lit up, and immediately started in at each other. They were heavy smokers, and I wasn't an hour into the arrangements before the ashtray on my desk was full of cigarette butts stubbed out in anger. They used the gesture of stubbing out a cigarette like an exclamation point at the end of a sentence, getting louder and more animated as our arrangement conference progressed. They couldn't agree on anything. The air was blue and thick with language and smoke.

The brothers' anger grew with the pile of stubbed butts until the ashtray couldn't hold one more butt. Brian screamed some obscenities at his brother and stormed out. Over the next two days I played mediator and got them to agree, for the sake of their mother, on a funeral that suited everyone.

In those days the world wasn't so "sue-happy" and I allowed booze in my funeral home. It was the typical Irish wake. They brought all sorts of food and drink and partied for most of the evening with music, singing, joking, and carrying on—the dead man lying in the parlor almost an afterthought. It was a big crowd, and the two brothers were pretty well behaved except for some yelling and pushing that was quickly broken up by friends. But they kept their distance from each other for the entire night. The wake ended and everyone left the party in good, drunken spirits.

The next morning the brothers showed up separately. Brian came first, escorting his mother. He reeked of cigarettes and whiskey and looked the part, too. He obviously hadn't shaved or combed his hair, and his eyes were bloodshot and had the look of a hunted animal about them. I escorted them into the private family room, got them settled, and greeted the rest of the guests as they arrived. James arrived much later wearing the same clothes he had worn the previous evening. He obviously hadn't been home. He too reeked of rye, and attached to his arm was a garishly dressed young lady whom he introduced to me as his girlfriend.

I escorted James and his girlfriend to the family room and outlined to the McSomething family how things would go that day so we would all be on the same page. Immediately, the two brothers started verbally sparring. I tried to nip it in the bud by saying, "Gents, could you please just behave today for the sake of your mother and in memory of your dead father?" That seemed to work. They stopped arguing and merely glowered at each other. Their mother sat silent, looking shell-shocked. I got the family seated right before service time and gave a colleague the task of getting the funeral started; I had other plans.

While the service was going on I wanted to embalm a body that had come in during the night. I went into the basement, where the prep room is, took off my coat and tie, put on a gown and pair of gloves. I knew that if I hurried I would be able to get done before the service ended and go back upstairs to say goodbye to everyone. It was wintertime, and in my area of the country you can't bury in the winter. Everyone gets stored in a vault until the spring thaw, which sometimes doesn't come until early June. I had just gotten the body undressed and was giving it a preliminary wash when the entire funeral home shook like it had been hit by a plane. *BOOM!*

I tore off my gloves and gown and rushed upstairs in my shirtsleeves to find a circle of people in the parlor yelling and screaming. I pushed my way to the center of the circle to find James standing over Brian. Brian was laid out on the floor, blood gushing from his nose. As I floundered into the circle James yelled, "Don't talk about my girl like that!" He circled his motionless opponent, shaking his bloody fist and ranting like a madman.

I knelt over Brian and slapped his face. "Hey! Can you hear me?" I yelled. Then I looked up at James, "Are you crazy?"

Brian opened his eyes.

"You all right?" I asked.

Brian shook his head, pushed me out of the way, and sat up. Bright red blood ran from his nose like a faucet, gushing down the front of his suit and onto the carpet.

James yelled, "You better stay down if you know what's good for you." He continued circling his prey, waving his bloody fists.

Brian ignored him and got unsteadily to his feet. He took a couple of tentative steps, before he spit a huge bloody loogie onto the carpet, put his dukes up, and said, "C'mon."

The crowd exploded in yells and jeers, and Brian took a mighty swing at his brother. It caught him in the arm, but with enough force that James reeled backwards into a lamp on a table, smashing both.

"Hey! Hey!" I yelled desperately at seeing my funeral home being destroyed. "Take it outside or I'm calling the cops!"

Surprisingly enough, the mob listened. A couple of burly men in leather jackets grabbed them and said. "You heard the man, lads, take your grievances outside." They marched them outside like truant children.

The crowd rushed outside, leaving only a crying Mrs. McSomething alone in the parlor with her dead husband. I was torn. I didn't know what to do. Console the widow, or try to break up the fight.

I ran outside.

There was at least a foot of snow on the ground and the two boys were out in the front lawn just swinging away. The clean, white snow was dotted with little crimson drops of blood. They were still going strong; I had never seen men take such hits before and still be able to stand. I rushed in to break it up but was intercepted by the burly arm of one of the men who had carried them outside. "Let them fight," was all he said to me.

I decided to listen to the giant, and stood and watched as Brian and James beat the—for lack of a better word—*shit* out of each other. Brian was wearing a black shirt but I could tell it was covered in blood by the way the sunlight reflected off the wetness saturating it. James was wearing a white shirt that looked like he had worn it while slaughtering a pig. They slowed down until, at the end, they were just taking wild swings at each other.

Finally, James landed a solid blow to Brian's jaw. Brian dropped into the snow and lay there motionless. James turned away from his conquest, tripped, and face-planted into the snow where he, too, remained motionless.

There they lay, two brothers, motionless in the bloody snow. The burly men carried them back into the parlor and propped them up on chairs; the crowd took their seats and the service resumed with someone saying prayers. The priest had left when the fight broke out.

At the end of the service, I had the casket bearers help me load the casket into the hearse for the ride over to the vault. It was a comical sight, the two brothers, side by side, dried blood covering their faces, James with his one eye swollen shut, and Brian with his broken nose carrying their father's casket. They looked like two whipped dogs.

I was glad to see the McSomethings go and decided that next time they called upon my services I would be too busy to accommodate them. Unfortunately, I still had to be around them when we buried their father after the spring thaw. I didn't relish that day, and in fact, dreaded it the rest of the winter.

On the day of the interment Brian and James showed up in the same car, smelling as they usually did, of booze, but strangely enough, the best of friends. They called each other "brother" during the short committal service and boasted of their drinking exploits the night before. I couldn't believe they were the same two people I had watched duke it out in front of my funeral home not four months prior.

I just couldn't resist. Before I left I asked Brian, "How did you get that scar over your eye?"

He grinned, revealing several missing teeth. "Fightin' James."

CHAPTER 33

Lucky

Contributed by a Texas Hold 'Em player

I remember the first funeral I was given to direct on my own after I graduated from mortuary school. It was a disaster...almost. But I'm Lucky. My real name is some God-awful albatross my parents shackled upon me, Chester. So you can see why I prefer my nickname to my real name. I got the name because, whether it be playing poker or nearly ruining a funeral, I can step into a dung pile and still come out smelling like a daisy.

I did my internship at McDaniel-Walsh. It is a prestigious old firm with the physical plant housed in a big old Victorian mansion. I lived on the third floor in a small dorm-type room. It's the type of room that's hot in the summer and cold in the winter, but I was just glad for a place to stay. My rent? The phone for the funeral home rang up in my room from 6:00 P.M. to 7:30 A.M. six nights a week; that's how I paid rent.

The funeral directors who worked for McDaniel-Walsh were considerably older than me and thought I was just a stupid kid. They couldn't be bothered with explaining anything to me. I think they thought I should instinctively know it all. Or maybe they thought that just by merely being in their presence I'd pick up their knowledge through osmosis. Either way, they didn't give me much responsibility at first. In fact, I was like their live-in janitor when I started, and I also had the pleasure of hearing them speak to me like I was retarded—loud and slow. "Chet"—they refused to call me Lucky because it was an "unprofessional" name—"can you *wax* the cars today?"

So I kept my head down and worked hard, and slowly, very slowly, they began giving me more responsibility.

One morning after I'd been at McD and W for about six months, the phone rang up in my attic apartment. It was Mark, one of the directors. He told me his wife had been rushed to the hospital during the night and he wouldn't be in to work that day. Could I take the funeral he had planned?

Could I? "Of course I can," I told him, excited at the prospect of actually doing some funeral directing.

He gave me directions to the church and cemetery and told me the pallbearers would meet me at the church to help me in.

"Do you know what to do?" Mark asked me.

"Yes, I know what to do."

"Chet, are you sure?" he repeated.

"Don't worry. Everything will be fine," I assured him.

He thanked me and hung up. I was ecstatic. This was my big chance to really prove myself and move up from my current custodial duties of polishing the brass ashtrays and replacing the urinal cakes. I ran out and loaded the funeral coach with everything I would need for church: floral stands, sign-in book, pedestals, makeup grip, automobile funeral tags, and the like. I left with plenty of time, but because I was relatively new to the area, and didn't travel very much outside the immediate area of the funeral home except to go to the grocery store or the occasional movie, I got on the freeway going in the wrong direction.

I didn't realize my mistake at first, because the exits on this particular freeway are so far and few between, but I finally noticed the exit numbers kept getting bigger. I was looking for an exit number that was supposed to be lower. *That's okay,* I told myself, *I'll just get off at the next exit and hop back on. I'll still be there in plenty of time.*

I drove and drove. At one point I contemplated driving over the grass median and getting in the southbound lanes, but it appeared there was a slight ditch and I had visions of getting the funeral coach stuck in the median and making the nightly news. I gripped the steering wheel and willed the next exit to come. It came and I took it. I drove up to the top of the off-ramp, hooked a left turn, and discovered there was no access to the southbound lanes of the freeway. That's when I began to panic. These were the days before cell phones or GPS navigation devices, and the exit I had gotten off at was for farm country. There weren't any gas stations I could inquire at, just fields. I had a choice. I could continue northbound on the freeway, or I could try to backtrack through the back roads until I linked up again with the freeway.

I gritted my teeth and kept driving, straight into farm country.

Twenty-five minutes after the funeral service was supposed to start I pulled up to the curb; my face was flushed and my nerves were frayed. I felt like my body would snap, I was so agitated. I had blown it. I had ruined my one big chance to prove myself. When this got back to Mark I was finished!

Forty-five people with arms folded glared at me as I threw the coach in park and killed the engine. I thought the knot in my stomach would jump right out my throat. I squeezed my eyes shut and bit my lower lip so hard I could taste blood inside my mouth, and then I took a deep breath and got ready for the reaming I was sure to receive. I threw open the door and was totally unprepared for what came.

The daughter of the deceased flew down the church stairs, pushing through the throng of furious faces. "My mother always said she'd be late to her own funeral! Oh, this is just perfect!" She stopped short and looked at me. "Who are you?"

"I'm Lucky. Mark's wife was rushed to the hospital last night so he sent me."

"Oh my, I hope his wife is all right!"

I assured her she was.

"And to think, his wife is in the hospital and Mark is still think-ing of my family, and having you arrive late so mother would be late. We laughed about her tardiness for a good while when I was in making the funeral arrangements. What a sweet man! He really did think of everything!"

"He's always thinking of others," I agreed.

"This just made the funeral *perfect*," the daughter stressed.

I just smiled.

We proceeded with the funeral, and the daughter couldn't thank me enough.

I accepted the praise with as much grace as I could muster that day. I couldn't seem to shake the feeling that I had dodged a bullet.

Two days after the funeral Mark approached me while I was painting the eaves of the portico. "The daughter of that funeral you took the other day called me."

"Oh?" I said, putting my paintbrush down.

He had a funny look on his face. "Thanked me for having you show up late because, I quote, 'Mother always said she'd be late to her own funeral.'"

"So she's happy then, I take it?"

He stared at me for a long time. I stared right back. Finally, he broke the silence. "You're lucky."

Yes, I am.

CHAPTER 34

Believe in the Butterfly

Contributed by a Young Republican

A founder of St. Patrick's Church, Connor McLeod, died. He was 103.

St. Patrick's Roman Catholic Church is a beacon on a desolate urban landscape, only illuminated once a year, the date of the death of the patron saint of Ireland. On that one day it becomes the epicenter of the city's focus, but when the green beer has dried up it's just another neo-Gothic structure in the neo-ghetto.

There was a time when St. Pat's was more than just a holiday icon, a time before the ethnic lines of delineation blurred and it was an all-Irish neighborhood. It was the time of Connor McLeod when the congregation was a thousand plus strong. The families of the original congregation have moved to the suburbs and the repentant souls that fill the pews on Sundays have shrunk to a pittance.

But when there is a death in the suburbs, the families want to return to their roots in the city, as in the case of Connor McLeod.

Connor's mother and father emigrated from Ireland in the late 19th century; Connor was born six months after their arrival, a product of their pilgrimage. He grew up in the all-Irish neighbor-

hood and lived there for most of his life until his health forced
him to relocate to a suburban rest home. Though he loved
St. Patrick's, in his older years he had resorted to attending daily
mass at a local parish. But upon his death, Connor's family
wanted him to be buried from the place of his youth, his home,
St. Patrick's.

Connor decided to die during one of the biggest heat waves
the region could remember. Even my father, a fixture in the community, was commenting how he couldn't remember the heat ever
being so bad. The elderly were urged to stay indoors, and the
power companies rejoiced at the bonanza. Of course, St. Pat's was
built before air conditioning, and the dwindling congregation's
coffers couldn't afford to retrofit the building with it. On the day
of Connor's Mass of Christian Burial every window and door to
the massive old church was thrown open. Somebody from the
church even resurrected a box of old reed fans, printed with the
logo Dumphy and Sons, Inc—something my grandfather had provided the church, no doubt.

The humid air hung heavy, stagnant, caught in the vaulted ceiling. The mass proceeded quickly as the congregation sat vigorously fanning themselves. The priest, a monsignor, and friend of
Connor's, celebrated the mass and prepared a special homily for
the day. I think the funeral analogy people are most familiar with
is likening our lives to the seasons—it seems to be a favorite of
the clergy—but on this day the Reverend Monsignor James Shannon likened Connor's life to the life of a butterfly. He described
Connor's life as a caterpillar, his death as the cocoon, and his rebirth into new life as a beautiful butterfly. It was a touching homily about Connor's life and his faith.

Just as Monsignor Shannon was wrapping up his homily, a
giant blue butterfly flew in through one of the open windows. It
sailed down a shaft of light and perched on the pall of the casket. The butterfly gently flapped its wings a couple of times before taking off. It floated lazily over the altar for a few seconds;

Monsignor's gaze fixed upon it and he faltered. As Monsignor collected himself and finished, the butterfly took off out the window.

It wasn't a big dramatic event. Even so, I wouldn't have believed it if I hadn't been sitting in the rear of the church and had witnessed it for myself.

My father nudged me. "Liam, did you see that?" he murmured.

"Yeah," I replied uneasily. "Freaky."

My father smiled at me in a knowing way.

I puzzled over the event as the mass wrapped up, and we processed to the cemetery, lowered Connor into his final resting place, and dropped the family off at their reception hall. *What had happened?*

There was no doubt in my mind *if* it had happened. It had happened. Everyone in the congregation, as well as the priest and my father, had witnessed the butterfly. What I was trying to make sense of was *what* had happened.

Was it a coincidence that Monsignor Shannon was talking about Connor's rebirth as a butterfly at the exact same moment a butterfly settled on Connor's casket? I don't put much stock in coincidences, but I saw the butterfly, and it moved me in a way I can't explain. I've come to the conclusion that the butterfly had nothing to do with coincidence, superstition, or religion. The butterfly was a sign of faith.

Though I'm not an overwhelmingly religious man, I do consider myself a deeply spiritual man—and spirituality is the root of all religions. What transcends religious borders and cultures is the belief, the *faith,* in the everlasting soul. The butterfly was affirming that faith. It was Connor saying to his family, "Though I'm dead, I live on."

And it wasn't hard to see how he lived on. His beautiful family sat in the first three pews in the church he helped found, and his undying faith in his God had allowed him the chance to say one last farewell.

I believe that how you, as a reader, accept this story will say a lot about your individual faith.

Whether you're Christian, Muslim, Hindu, agnostic, or an atheist, if you haven't had the chance yet in your life, or are too scared, I urge you to take that first step. It's only the tiniest of steps.

Believe in the butterfly.

CHAPTER 35

Continuum

Contributed by an actor

T here's a beautiful old cemetery in my area that reminds me of a scene in a movie. Every time I drive through the gates of Manhattan Heights Cemetery, I think of *Rain Man*. I'm sure everybody has seen that movie. It stars Tom Cruise and Dustin Hoffman and won the Oscar for best picture in 1988.

In the scene where Cruise's character goes to meet his brother in the institution for the first time, the camera pans the oak-lined driveway. This is how Manhattan Heights is; roadways lined with giant old oaks stand like timeless sentinels, flanked by rolling fields where grave markers nestle in the perfectly trimmed grass. The cemetery is a lovely, tranquil place.

When I was just starting my apprenticeship, I was given the task of going out to Manhattan Heights to do a headstone rubbing. It was a clear, sunny, spring day. Everything was green, and the leaves on the trees were full, causing the sunlight to fall onto the cemetery drive in intermittent pools. I cruised through the gates slowly, enjoying the weather and the solitude. As I crested the hill, I saw an old woman standing over a fresh mound. The funeral flowers piled on the mound weren't wilted yet, so I knew the grave was only a day or two old.

The woman was alone, and I assumed she was the wife of the deceased. Despite the warmth of the afternoon, she wore a heavy wool skirt and sweater. She held one withered hand to her forehead as though she had a headache, motionless as she looked at the patch of freshly disturbed earth.

A woman pushing a baby emerged from an intersecting drive and turned towards the elderly woman. The mother was young looking, twenty-seven or twenty-eight would be my guess, and based on her pace, was simply out for a leisurely stroll. She wasn't visiting anyone today. The baby was swaddled in a pink cotton blanket. I thought it strange for a woman to be walking her child in a cemetery, but I guess it's a better place than most. It's quiet, usually clean, and there isn't much traffic.

As the mother and daughter passed the elderly woman, neither party seemed to notice the other. But, I, in my car, saw the continuum of life. Grandmother. Mother. Daughter.

At one point in time, not in the too distant past, the grandmotherly woman had been that little girl being pushed in the stroller. She had blinked, and now she was burying a husband. Her spring has quickly turned to winter, and another spring was fast approaching.

Time doesn't wait. Cherish every day of your life.

CHAPTER 36

The Prodigal Son

Contributed by a jazz pianist

T here is a natural order in the world. Sometimes the order is broken and the parent is burdened with the task of burying the child. Of all the things I have to deal with in my profession, this situation is always the toughest. It can happen organically, accidentally, or self-destructively. But whichever way you slice it, it's still a bitter pill to swallow.

The story of the prodigal son is as old as written history, and I see it re-enacted too many times every year. Usually, it's the wayward son or daughter coming home to mourn the loss of a parent, but sometimes it's the prodigal son coming home on a flight for his own funeral; a flight in which I pick him up at the cargo bay at the airport, load him into the hearse, take him back to my funeral parlor, and lay him out for his parents to come mourn him.

A woman who we'll call "Casey" contacted me a year ago. Casey's son, "Jeff," had died of a drug overdose while out in Las Vegas.

When Casey called me, she needed someone to listen.

"I was a single mom," she said. "I dropped out of high school at the age of 17 to have Jeff. It was a bad situation. The man that impregnated me disappeared and my parents disowned me. I was left homeless with an infant."

I made a sound of sympathy and she continued, "I earned my GED, got a job with the state, and even managed to buy a home, although it wasn't in a section of town that was that good. I had to work a lot to keep my son and myself afloat and I wasn't always there to keep an eye on little Jeffrey. He started running with the wrong people and getting messed up. Drugs."

"Oh Jeez," I said.

"I didn't watch him close enough. It's my fault. All of this... is my fault."

"You can't blame yourself."

She ignored the comment. "He dropped out of high school and lived at home for a couple of years. He'd disappear for weeks on end and I'd never know where he was or even if he was—" She paused. "And I never knew where he got money, even though I had my suspicions. Jeffrey never worked. I begged him to get help. Really, I did. I begged and begged but he wouldn't listen. He'd always say, 'Ma, I don't need help,' but he did. He needed help."

I kept quiet and let her talk.

"A couple of short stints in prison for drug charges and petty burglary didn't straighten him out, but a laced batch of heroin that nearly killed him did. That overdose convinced him to get into rehab. Best thing he ever did. Jeffrey came out a changed person. He got a girlfriend, finished high school, *not* the GED thing like I did, actual high school, and held a steady job... for 18 months."

"Oh no," I said.

"Yeah. The high was too appealing. Jeffrey went back to it and it was worse than before. Way worse. I just couldn't stand it anymore, so I threw him out of my house," she said matter-of-factly. "I never heard from him again. It's been almost a year since I threw him out. And then yesterday I got this call from this medical guy out in Vegas—" Her voice cracked.

I offered her some comforting words and assured her we'd get her son back so she could give him a proper burial. Her parting words to me that day before she hung up were, "I don't even have any idea how he got out there or what he was doing there."

Casey didn't have a lot of money, but I was able to work with her so we could give Jeff a quiet, dignified burial. Casey and three of her friends were the only ones at the service in my chapel. After the minister performed his brief service, I ushered everyone out, leaving just Casey. She stood before Jeff's casket, her trembling hand touching his. He looked peaceful. His long hair hid the autopsy incisions, as did the collared flannel shirt. Casey had been very calm up until this point, but now she broke down sobbing. I stood next to her and put my arm around her and held her gently.

Casey didn't curse her son, or denounce him, but merely wept for a couple of minutes before digging into her large purse. She pulled out a bag of marijuana and threw it in, followed by bags of God-knows-what-else, a small bong, a couple of homemade pipes, some syringes without needles, and other things I didn't even recognize.

"I cleaned out his room," she said. "Leave them in there. If he wanted his drugs so much, then he can take them with him. Close it."

I closed the lid. Casey composed herself and walked out to the lobby. We embraced in the lobby and she said, "Thank you for letting me put all this to rest."

Later in the day I drove Jeff out to the cemetery. The men from the vault company helped me place him on the lowering device, and without a soul in the world who knew Jeffrey watching, I lowered his casket into the gaping hole in the earth.

The prodigal son had come home.

Broken families, fractured families, black sheep, and estrangement; unfortunately, I've seen it all. Is there really an issue that is so great you can't mend that fence? Reach out. At the end of the day, family is all you have in this world.

CHAPTER 37

Duel at High Noon

Contributed by a guitarist

I had never heard of a gun battle disrupting a funeral until the day I found myself in the middle of one.

It was a spring day, clear and sunny, and after the entire winter of hiding in church vestibules during funeral services, I took advantage of the beautiful day to sit outside and kill time. The service was Orthodox, and those are usually good to go for at least an hour or more.

That church is in the city. I was lounging on the wide stone steps, keeping an eye out for straggling mourners, leafing through *Car and Driver,* and not really paying attention to the passers-by, when some yelling caught my attention. On the corner of the block, about one hundred fifty feet from where I was sitting, two men were arguing. Their faces inches away from each other, they both gesticulated wildly, obviously irate. Their argument was more interesting than my magazine, and I put it down to watch. They shouted and pointed for a few more seconds and then stormed away from each other, the argument seemingly over. I started to go back to my magazine when I saw guns appear.

The firearms were drawn from under their billowy white tee shirts—almost the way a magician produces a dove. I'm not too up-to-date on my firearms, so I have no idea what type of guns they were except that they were black. It was like a scene from an old western film. The two stood about fifteen feet apart, menacing each other with their weapons for what seemed to be a millennium, but was probably only a second before they just *unloaded*. They fired and fired, sparks spitting from the muzzles of the pistols, until the slides locked back. Gun smoke swirling around them, they looked down at themselves, stupefied to be unhurt, and within seconds of the cease-fire, took off like frightened jackrabbits in opposite directions.

I sat on the steps, stunned, as the smell of cordite stung my nostrils. *Did I just see a gun battle?* I asked myself. *No!* Shootouts were things on the front page of the local section, things of the night, things of abstraction. Shootouts didn't happen in broad daylight...outside a funeral!

While I was still trying to process the scene that had just unfolded before me, an unmarked police car appeared from nowhere. It was joined seconds later by two marked prowlers, a fourth, and then a fifth. One of the initial officers to respond at the scene ran by and yelled to me, "Nobody comes out of that church!"

His order spurred me out of my trance and I hopped up to man the church doors.

The mourners, having heard so many gunshots in such close proximity, had all made a beeline for the door. My partner and I, along with the limo driver, were at the big wooden doors forcibly holding them closed. I felt like an actor in some ridiculous movie, holding these giant castle-like doors closed against the pandemonium inside. The priest bullied his way to the front of the crowd and I conveyed the situation to him. He managed to get everyone settled down to the point where there was no more shouting, but they still stood just inside the front doors, milling like cattle, ready to stampede. They weren't settling back down for a funeral when a war was raging outside.

The police cars were joined by a helicopter and two K-9 units as well as several bicycle and motorcycle cops. They searched for about a half hour, but to no avail. I gave a brief statement about what I had seen and the police finally gave us the okay to empty the church. We processed on to the cemetery and the priest did his best to include at the graveside the parts of the liturgy missed in the church.

I checked the paper the next day and it mentioned the shooting. I guess they never did catch those two men. Not to be glib or anything, but perhaps those two men would benefit from a membership to a local shooting range.

CHAPTER 38

Wives and Girlfriends

Contributed by a veteran

I f there is one life lesson I have learned as an undertaker, it's this: the lies and secrets we maintain in life cannot be perpetuated in death. There is an old saying that goes, "Dead men tell no tales." That's true, but the dead also can't keep a secret. Whether it is a man's secret stack of *Playboy* magazines, a couple's titillating photos that were never meant to be shared with others, or a spouse's secret bank account, it all floats to the surface once the dead person protecting the secret dies. Many a person has told me of the discrete removal of certain objects from their friend's or sibling's house before the parents or children go in to clean it out. But aside from objects, stuff that maybe we shouldn't have or would be embarrassed to admit owning are the *people.*

The most common thing I see involving the secrets of the living and dead is the illicit sexual relationship. After a death relationships, which were previously buried in the shadows, are thrown into the light of day for all to see. When the secretkeeper is dead, so is the secret. It's sad when a good man's or woman's name is tarnished after they have died because some information floats to the surface, but it's human nature to have secrets, and it's something I've seen too many times.

Consider the situation of a man with a wife and girlfriend; or a woman with a husband and boyfriend. Man dies. Come the day of the funeral, wife and children are sitting in the front row on one side and girlfriend is on the other side. Sometimes the girlfriend makes a scene. Sometimes the wife makes a scene. Sometimes it's amicable. Either way, the girlfriend who was previously unknown, or only whispered about behind closed doors, is thrust into public display. Is it a disgrace to the dead man? I don't have an answer for that. That's a question you'd have to ask the dead man; I'm not one to judge the state of his marriage and infidelities.

I know what you're wondering, and, no, the girlfriend usually doesn't have the sagacity to stay away from her boyfriend's funeral. After all, it is the funeral of somebody she loves. Would you stay away from the funeral of somebody you loved? I didn't think so.

Now consider the other situation, a man with a girlfriend and a dead wife; or a woman with a boyfriend and dead husband. Wife dies. Girlfriend comes to wife's funeral to support her boyfriend (and possibly future hubby). In fact, I just had a funeral not too long ago when the couple hadn't been married very long. It was under two years. The wife died suddenly. The husband was ruined. Absolutely ruined. I haven't seen anyone that distraught in a good while. So it was really surprising to me when his girlfriend showed up at the funeral. Don't get me wrong, she wasn't obvious about it, but I could tell by the way she touched him (and some things I overheard) that she was his girlfriend. What was so puzzling to me was that this man was so grief-stricken I would have thought they had a perfect marriage. Obviously, it wasn't so perfect that Mr. X wasn't stepping outside his marital vows.

I think the kicker of my little relationship sightings was when a husband and wife died in a tragic car wreck. On the day of the funeral, sitting in the front pew opposite the children were the boyfriend and girlfriend of the couple! I found out when I was making the arrangements that "mom and dad couldn't stand each other." But I had no idea how complex their lives were. Apparently, the children knew about the affairs and each parent knew about the other's partner and was okay with the situation as long as it wasn't out in the open. Their marriage had slid into a marriage of convenience.

I'm not trying to say everyone is a philandering jerk. I just want to remind everyone to think about how you want to be remembered. Once you're dead, there is no covering the little lies and secrets, and the truth has a nasty habit of finding its way into a funeral.

CHAPTER 39

The World Record Holder

Contributed by a volunteer in the Big Brother Program

I definitely hold the world record for having done the most embarrassing things (that's right, *things*, plural) at work. I'm not talking about running out of gas on the freeway, splitting your pants and having nothing to change into, or falling asleep during an important meeting. All those things are embarrassing to a certain degree, but I'm talking about hitting the point where you want to crawl deep into a very dark hole and die. The type of embarrassment where you get heart palpitations and your mind goes blank and you can only focus on crawling into that hole. I'm sure everyone reading this has had moments of embarrassment, but see if they compare to a couple of my more glorious moments as the world's most embarrassing funeral director.

I'll preface the first incident by saying I spilled an entire cup of coffee down the widow's dress the night of the wake. But that's minor and can be solved with profuse apologies and a dry cleaner. If that were the worst thing that happened to me, I'd thank my lucky stars, but *the* incident happened while I was leading the funeral procession. The decedent was a pillar of the community, loved by all, and hated by none. He had quite a turnout for his send-off and there were at least fifty cars processing to the burial. The cemetery is in the next town over—a place I have been to many times during my career—but I was unaware there was road construction going on that day. The road I was planning on taking was blocked and I was forced to detour around it. I got hopelessly lost and led the entire procession down a dead end street.

You can imagine how I felt when I came to the barrier and had to do a three-point turn in the hearse, wait for the limo to do a five-point turn, and then wait for everyone else to turn their cars around and get back on their way. I finally found the cemetery by the grace of God, and let me tell you, I felt a lot of pairs of eyes on me that day!

It wasn't too long after the dead-end-street incident (as my colleagues like to call it) that I decided to go for another Hallmark embarrassing moment. We were a little busy on a particular day and I made funeral arrangements with two families. I am generally very careful about making copious notes and keeping everything separate, but when I went to order the casket engraving for the first family, I put down the first name of the wrong man. I didn't realize it when I faxed the order in. I didn't realize it when I checked the proof. I even didn't realize it when the casket arrived and I put the man in it. In my mind I had correctly matched their first and last names.

We had had the wake in the funeral home; celebrated the Mass of Christian Burial, and what I had done didn't dawn on me until I invited the widow up to the casket at the cemetery. "Do you like the engraving?" I asked, hand on her back.

"That's not my husband's name!" she wailed.

I felt about six inches big that day. I postponed the burial, and ordered a new casket lid. But those two incidents can't even hold a candle to the one incident that won me the title of having the "Most Embarrassing Moment in the World." It went something like this:

I get a death call. "Mom" has passed.

I tell them I'll be right over.

Of course, I stepped in dog poop in the front yard and didn't notice until I managed to track it all over the house. It was a mess. Of course, it was a white carpet. Did I cut my losses and let another funeral director handle the call? No! I pressed on.

The family came into the funeral home the next day, and after many, many apologies—I hope you see a pattern emerging—and insisting I hire a carpet cleaning company, I made the funeral arrangements with them. The family left and I started making the necessary calls to organize the funeral. One of my employees came in and started asking me questions about something and I got sidetracked. Later, when I went back over my notes, I made a mental checklist of everything I had done (or thought I had done) and everything I had to do. I finished making the necessary arrangements and left for the day.

Three days later we had a viewing in church followed by the funeral service. Everything went perfectly. After the service, my colleague and I got all the cars lined up, and we hopped into the hearse and headed for the cemetery. It is one of those big corporate memorial parks that are extremely well run and maintained, and because of that, it is a popular destination for the local dearly departed. Following a nice twenty-minute ride from the church, I pulled into the gates expecting a cemetery lead car to escort us to the grave. No cemetery lead car waited.

That's not a big deal. Sometimes the lead car gets tied up or is running late. So I headed off through the sprawling cemetery in the direction I thought the grave was, looking for the tent. We drove and drove through the miles of cemetery road, until I turned to my colleague and said, "This is ridiculous. Let's just go to the cemetery office and find out where the grave is. Maybe we can get someone to take us over there." I led the procession back through the cemetery and to the office, where I jumped out and ran in.

The cemetery secretary recognized me as I walked through the door. "Oh hi, Rob. What brings you here today?"

I looked at her peculiarly and replied, "The Allen funeral."

"Who?"

"The interment I've got here today."

She looked at me for a second and said, "We only had one on the books for today and it's already come in."

As I uttered the words, "What are you talking about?" it hit me. *I hadn't ordered the grave!* I could tell by the look on her face she was thinking the exact same thing. At that point, for a fleeting few moments, I honestly considered just slipping out the back door and hitchhiking home. But instead I said, "How quickly can you set up a mock site?" I asked her.

"I'll call the guys right now. Give us fifteen minutes."

"You're a lifesaver!"

As I walked out to the idling procession stretching out thirty cars down the cemetery drive, a thousand lies swirled through my head, but were interrupted by the pastor rolling down his car window and shouting none-too-kindly, "What's the hold-up? I've got other things to do today!"

I sidled up to his window and growled, "Take it easy. There's going to be a slight delay."

Obviously agitated, he shouted at me, "I told you I could do this funeral if it was over by one o'clock and it's one now!"

"Look," I snapped at him, "if you want to leave, go ahead. I've got the Book of Common Prayer in the hearse. I'll say the interment rites."

If looks could have killed I would have been dead and buried right there. He emitted a *humph,* crossed his arms, and stared straight ahead. I took that to mean he was going to wait.

I strolled back another car and motioned for the son of the deceased to get out of his car.

"What's the hold-up?" he asked me.

He was a really nice guy, and I decided honesty was the best policy no matter how stupid it made me look. *Imagine, one of the biggest parts of my job—ordering the grave—and I can't even remember to do that!* My face was scarlet and I thought my heart would explode out of my chest when I said, "Look, Brad, to be totally honest with you, I forgot to order the grave opening, so they're arranging a false setup. Once everyone leaves I'll wait around until they dig the grave and put your mother in."

He chuckled. "That's no problem, Rob. Don't feel bad."

"Well, I—"

Brad interrupted me. "Just last week I accidentally sent a shipment to the wrong location."

"This is a little different," I protested. Once again, I felt about six inches tall. "And not nearly as embarrassing."

"Hardly. I sent a shipment of beef, the holy cow, to an Indian restaurant. Big customer. My boss was less than pleased."

I felt better and laughed a little. "That sounds bad, but believe me. I am the king of embarrassment. I could tell you some stories."

"So could I," Brad said and rolled his eyes with an *I-know-what-you-mean* look.

"But this is inexcusable—"

"Like I said, it's no big deal. You've done a lot for my family in the past couple of days. You're allowed a mistake or two once in a while." He pounded me on the back. "We'll just hang tight until you're ready to roll. By the way, once you've finished up, you're welcome to come back to the country club and have lunch with us."

"*Er*, thanks?" I stammered.

When I climbed back into the hearse my colleague looked at me and said, "How'd it go?"

"Considering the fact that we're in the cemetery with his mother and no place to put her, he's pretty calm." I paused. "He invited us to lunch after we finally get his mother buried."

My colleague laughed. "Sometimes I think you have a horseshoe up your ass."

"I'll tell you this much. I'm not going to that luncheon. I'm going to find a very small, dark hole and crawl into it and stay there for a very long time."

After we wrapped things up at the grave and the family was leaving, I walked them back to their cars. Brad, as gracious as a human could ever be, sidled up to me. "So Rob, are you going to join us at the luncheon and regale me with reasons why you, and not I, hold the crown for embarrassment?"

As if to prove my point, I tripped over a memorial marker and face-planted.

CHAPTER 40

Third from Right

Contributed by a car enthusiast

I dressed up a woman like she was going out for Halloween when I wasn't supposed to...but not really. It's complicated. Let me explain.

I always ask the family for a photo of the deceased if it's a woman. The photo helps with makeup and hairstyling. Men generally don't require a photo. You don't want them to look like they have makeup on so you just use a little color to give them a ruddy complexion. But with women you need to know what colors to use where, how much makeup they used, and what type.

A woman named Karen died and her family came in to make arrangements. When I asked about the clothes, the family told me that Karen's best friend would be bringing them by the following day. I reminded them to have the neighbor bring in a photo of Karen so the hair stylist would know how to do her hair.

The following day, the friend brought in Karen's clothes and a photo. The photo had obviously been taken some time ago, perhaps in the late seventies or early eighties. It was a photo of eight women who were obviously at a party. They were lined up in front of a fireplace; all bore the silly expressions of women who had indulged in too many libations and gossip over the course of the evening. I commented on what a great picture it was and the neighbor informed me that the photo was of the founding members of their neighborhood garden club. She added that she was the only living member left of the original group. We talked a little about her departed friends, and I could tell she loved reminiscing about them. As she was leaving, I remembered I had failed to ask which one was the decedent. I called after the neighbor, "Which one is Karen?"

"Third from the right," she replied and ducked out the front door.

I was pleased that the woman in the photo enjoyed color, style, and fashion. Even though thirty years ago she was in her middle forties, she looked great. She was fit and tan, and leaning on her two friends flanking her, grinning a silly drunken grin. She had great big black eyelashes and light blue eye shadow topped off by a great big beehive hairdo that was Lucille Ball red.

The poor woman must have had a rough time near the end because she didn't look much like her old self. Her flamboyant red hair had turned gray and she had let it grow down to her waist. I called the family and got permission to dye the hair to the color in the photo. They assured me they loved that photo. In fact, their exact words were, "That's *her*. Do whatever you can to make her look like she did in that photo."

I did.

Unfortunately, the dress they brought in was lackluster compared to the fashionable empire style diamond print mini-dress in the photo. The pastel colored short skirt in the photo featured her muscular legs, and the mint colored sleeveless blouse showcased her ample bosom. The dress the neighbor had brought in was a shapeless brown thing, not even fit for a woman of such style. To say it had no pizzazz would be an understatement; it looked like a monk's robe. I picked up a mauve silk scarf at Goodwill and a big belt that I placed high around her waist in the typical seventies style to dress her up a little.

She was beginning to look like the photo.

Once the hair stylist dyed her hair, trimmed it up a bit, and styled it in a beautiful beehive hairdo, she looked *almost* like her old self. I added some fake eyelashes, thick mascara, and blue eye shadow to complete her makeover, but something was missing. I wiped off the burgundy colored lipstick the friend had brought in and reapplied a loud, light pink lipstick just like she wore in the photo.

Perfect! I thought, stepping back and taking a look at the finished product. *The family is going to love the way she turned out!*

The next day the members of the family came in before the viewing began. I assembled them in the lobby and took them all in. The two daughters and son walked up to the casket and I heard a collective gasp followed by a loud, "What the hell?"

I rushed up to see what was the matter and the eldest daughter turned to me and pointed a finger at me and wailed, "What did you do to my mother? She looks like a clown!"

"I—I—I tried to make her look like the picture! I'm sorry if you're not pleased—"

The son roared, "We sure as hell aren't—"

One of the daughters cut him off, "But her hair!"

"You told me I could dye it like the picture!" I protested.

"You idiot," the son yelled. "It's red!"

Then it dawned on me. "I'm sorry," I said. "But your mother's friend told me your mother was third from the right."

I pointed to the picture I had left lying at the foot of the casket.

"Oh God," the son groaned, looking at the picture, "she's third from the left! You made her look like Mrs. MacDonnell!"

I rushed over to get a closer look at the photo. The woman third from the left, though looking nothing like the decedent, had longish blond hair and wore a simple floral print dress. And though she had the same silly grin as Mrs. MacDonnell, she wore none of the thick makeup. In fact, she wore none at all, except for a trace of burgundy colored lipstick.

The neighbor who had given me the photo walked up to the casket to see what all the commotion was about and recoiled in revulsion. "Who is that?" she demanded.

"You told the undertaker mom was third from the right," the son said quietly.

The look of horror that crossed the woman's face was almost comical. I could tell she wanted to run and hide. "Oh dear," was all she could utter. She looked at me with a look that said, *Did I?*

I nodded at her solemnly and put my arm around her shoulders. "Don't worry," I assured the three children and neighbor. "I can fix this. Give me fifteen minutes." I ushered them out of the parlor and re-appeared twenty minutes later, my shirt soaked through with perspiration. She looked as close to the picture as I could muster, except her hair was the wrong color for the viewing.

The next day she was third from left. And her hair was blond.

In Our Private Lives

Do undertakers have a private life? Good question...I don't know. Maybe you can answer that question after reading this section and weighing in on some of the contributors' answers. But to be a little more objective, let me clarify.

As the handlers of the dead, we don't get off Christmas Day, New Year's, or the 4th of July. We may have some hours to devote to our family on those holidays, or on Sundays, but if you call us we'll be over. We have 24-hour business hours. We never close for re-modeling, have a snow day, or cancel events due to inclement weather. We socialize with a pager attached to the hip and sleep with a phone next to our bed, and, as you'll see in one of mine, "The First Date," we sacrifice love for work.

I guess you could say that our private lives are inextricably intertwined with our professional lives. That kind of commingling can lead to some...odd, private moments. Ken still has the feather in his desk that you'll read about in "Feathers and Fridges."

Not only do we eat, sleep, and breathe our ministry—our calling—some of us, hell, most of us work with family and live at the funeral home. Can you imagine living where you work? Pitching a tent in your cubicle? It would be the same thing! Because it's often hard to walk that line separating our business and personal lives, it is important for us to have activities outside the profession. That's why we identified contributors by their outside hobbies or interests. And believe it or not, we do have interests outside of our thanatological (translation: death and dying) pursuits.

The stress of the job can sometimes lead to strained family situations and personal problems. Ken is a perfect example. The daily stresses of running the mortuary he started almost fifteen years ago gradually built up and manifested themselves in a disease that is common in a lot of high-stress jobs—alcoholism. In a recent conversation we had, he was recounting stories about both his grandmothers, who sadly died during the writing of this book. He told me one grandmother, to whom this book is dedicated, told him before he started in the profession, "If you're going to be a funeral director, make sure you watch your drinking. Every funeral director I know is a raging alcoholic!" After their deaths, Ken had an epiphany and started treatment. He is now taking one day at a time and has a new, positive outlook on his life and profession.

I hope that if you take anything away from this book, it's a new outlook on those of us that ply the death trade. When we come home every night (or, in some cases, upstairs in the funeral home) and take off our hats and kick our feet up, we're just the same as you . . . but call us, and we'll gladly put that hat right back on for you.

CHAPTER 41

Feathers and Fridges

Contributed by a community philanthropist

I began handling Mrs. Bingen's family about ten years ago when her son unexpectedly died. I just happened to be assigned to make the funeral arrangements that day. It was a tough funeral, the kind that tears at the emotional fabric of the soul. Tragic death. Young man. Mrs. Bingen and I connected on an emotional level during the time we were together. It's never a joyous occasion when you need the services of a member of my profession, but it's nice to find someone you can trust to make sure your loved one is taken care of properly. Mrs. Bingen found me and from that point on I've been handling all of Mrs. Bingen's family.

Those ten years since her son's death were tough ones. I handled her parents, an aunt, and finally, her husband. I think the strain of all the deaths combined with her advancing age may have affected her mind. Towards the end of that ten-year stretch, I really didn't even know her anymore; she got a little loopy.

One morning I pulled into the parking lot of the funeral home and I could've sworn I saw Mrs. Bingen leaving in the backseat of a taxi. I waved. The woman in the taxi didn't. I pushed the thought from my mind and went inside.

"Hi Fiona," I greeted the receptionist as I usually did.

"Er, Ken," she said. "I have something for you." She held out a battered shoebox.

"What is it?" I demanded. I was suspicious it was some kind of prank.

"Some strange lady just dropped it off. Said you'd know what to do with it." Fiona shrugged.

"What was her name?"

"Mrs. Birmingham, I think." She shrugged again. Fiona shrugs a lot, like she's never sure about anything. "She was talking really fast, and not making too much sense. Kept saying, 'Ken will know what to do.'"

"Was her name Bingen?"

"Could have been." She shrugged. "Like I said, she was talking really fast."

I took the shoebox and took a peek inside. There, lying in a bed of crumpled newspaper, was a dead green bird. It was pretty good sized, maybe the length of my hand. I showed the contents of the shoebox to Fiona.

"Eww," she said and wrinkled her nose. "A dead bird!" The tone of her voice suggested that this woman had brought a dead bird to a bakery instead of a mortuary. I didn't bother pointing that out to Fiona.

"Did she say what she wanted me to do with this?" I asked Fiona, who had now pushed her chair back from her desk to get as far away from the shoebox and the offending bird as possible.

She offered me one of her patented shrugs. "She said she was moving to Illinois and that, 'Ken will—'"

I finished the sentence, "Know what to do with it. Okay, okay, I get it."

I called the most recent number I had for Mrs. Bingen. The number had been disconnected. So I pulled up files from the past ten years when I had handled her relatives and found some phone numbers. I called a couple of Mrs. Bingen's distant relatives listed in the files. Nobody had a forwarding phone number or address, but I left my phone number with each of them. I had no idea what she wanted me to do with her bird, but I knew I'd hear from her eventually, so I left the bird in the box and labeled it and put it on a shelf in our walk-in refrigerator and kind of forgot about it. We got busy at work, I started some remodeling in the house, and one of my dogs cut his paw on a piece of glass and needed twenty stitches.

About six weeks after Mrs. Bingen dropped her dead bird off, something jogged my memory and I remembered the bird in the refrigerator. I couldn't leave it there. If the State Board happened to do one of their inspections, they would fine the funeral home for having an animal in the refrigerator, so I went down and retrieved my little charge. The bird at this point was mummified. I took it home in its shoebox, put it on the windowsill in my garage, and once again forgot about it.

Another six weeks passed, or maybe more, and I arrived and greeted Fiona in the same manner I always did.

"Ken, got a message for you," she said. "Mrs. Birmingham called."

"Bingen?"

She shrugged. "Maybe. She sounds nuts."

"She leave a number?"

"No. She just said that someone would be here tomorrow to pick the bird up and drive it to Illinois so she could bury it in a pet cemetery near her new house."

I laughed, relieved, thankful I hadn't taken the initiative of having the bird cremated or burying it myself. "Alright. Thanks, Fiona. We get all kinds, don't we?"

"We sure do," she replied.

I wrote myself a note, and when I got home that night I put the note under my keys so I would remember to retrieve the bird before I left for work the next day. In the morning I went out to the garage; the door was slightly ajar, almost like it hadn't closed properly. *That's strange*, I thought, and hoisted up the door. My two dogs greeted me from inside the garage. They weren't supposed to be in the garage. The chocolate Lab ran over, panting and wagging his tail. He was pleased with himself. A green feather hung out of the side of his mouth.

I snatched the green feather from Remus's jowls and stared at it, incredulous.

Frantic, I ran over to the window and found the shoebox on the ground. It was torn to shreds. My two little angels must have discovered the open door during the night and raided the place. When I picked up the tattered shoebox, the smarter of the two, Vixen, a Rhodesian Ridgeback, cowered in the corner. I was sure she was the one that led the raid, and she was ashamed. Not Remus, he's the mischievous (and stupid) one. Remus pranced and danced around me happy as a lark, almost as if to say, *Yeah, it was me. I ate that bird and it was delicious!*

"No!" I cried. I had saved the stupid bird for this woman for the better part of three months and my two dogs had ruined it! Why hadn't I put the bird in my car last night? Why hadn't Mrs. Bingen called a day earlier? Why hadn't one of the workmen closed the garage properly? Visions of cremating my two little angels flashed briefly before my eyes, but looking at their cute faces, Vixen's shame, and Remus's sheer idiocy made me forgive them. There was only one thing I could do. I hopped in my car and sped off toward the pet store.

Halfway there I realized there was no way I could buy Tweety bird and then break its neck. I loved animals too much. So I altered my course and drove the back roads looking for some kind of road kill bird to put in the shoebox.

I searched and searched and found no dead birds on the side of the road. Then I went home and searched through my dogs' droppings hoping to find some evidence of the bird. There was none. Defeated, I went to work and tried to think up a lie to tell the driver who was coming for the bird.

The driver never came for the dead bird, and I never heard from Mrs. Bingen again. To this day, I'm still not sure, what I would have said to the driver when he or she arrived. But I still keep the green feather I snatched from Remus's mouth in my desk drawer.

CHAPTER 42

Till Death

Contributed by a Harley rider

U nfortunately, the occasion on which I had to meet one of the strongest, most caring people I have ever known, as well as someone I easily call my best friend, involved the death of that person's husband. Tragic, yes, the husband's death, but in reality—not to get too philosophical—we're all actively dying. Some of us just slip into the great beyond with greater suddenness than others, and Kristy's husband was one of those unfortunates.

It was the luck of the draw, if you can call it that. I showed up for work one fine Monday after a fantastic weekend riding in the Mojave. The weather that morning was perfect and that always puts me in a good mood in the morning. Nothing ruined a day like having to drive my *car* to work.

On this Monday I was assigned to make funeral arrangements with the Morris family. The widow was coming in at ten o'clock. The decedent, a man, had died suddenly the day before of a suspected heart attack. His body was at the local hospital. The case was being referred to the medical examiner. I stowed my leather jacket and helmet in my locker, put on my tie—I couldn't ride my Soft Tail in good conscience with a tie on—and gathered my papers.

The woman who walked through the front door of the mortuary was far too young to be a widow. I'd guess her to be in her early thirties and she appeared to be quite tall, though it was hard to tell for she was leaning heavily on another, older, woman. Normally, I would assume the older woman to be the widow. But it was the younger woman, her wide, soft facial features distorted by emotional turmoil, which cued me to the fact that she was the widow. I strode up to the pair and introduced myself.

"Mrs. Morris. I am so sorry for your loss. My name is Geary and I'll be handling the funeral arrangements for your husband."

My name is a good icebreaker, especially in tough situations like this. My real name is Rudolph, but everyone calls me Geary because I'm such a little gear head.

Both women liked that and I even drew a smile out of the widow, especially when I told them how the deaf old ladies that call the mortuary always ask for Gary.

Mrs. Morris brushed a lock of blond hair out of her face, stared me right in the eye, and said, "Please Gary, call me Kristy, and I'll do my best to remember your name."

The three of us laughed.

I don't know how to explain it other than we clicked. Yes, we had instant chemistry—I don't mean romantic chemistry—but a kindred spirit kind of chemistry.

I invited them into my office and began the delicate business of making her husband's final plans. During the course of the arrangement process, I found out that Kristy was a 38-year-old mother of two girls aged 11 and 13. And I, always an open ear, heard her life story and cried and laughed along the way. She was an orphan, raised in various foster homes around the Catskill Mountain region before going to beauty school. She met her husband when he sat down in her chair one day. A month later they were married. Kristy's husband had been a sergeant in the army and had just been stationed at Fort Irwin two months ago after spending the past ten years at Fort Bragg in North Carolina—the place she called "home." Both of his parents were dead, she had no family to speak of, and she knew nobody here in California. The elderly woman who accompanied her was her next-door neighbor, Mrs. Logan, who had known Kristy for two months.

Normally, I can sympathize with my families, but with Kristy I could *empathize*. Being a quasi-orphan myself, I could relate to her feelings of isolation; I was an only child. My father committed suicide when I was nine, and my mother was locked up for drugs shortly thereafter. I was raised by my maternal grandmother, who though loving, I know now was showing the early signs of Alzheimer's when I showed up on her doorstep at age twelve. So, other than my German shepherd, Chloe, I have no other family in the world. My grandmother died two years prior and last I heard, my mother was slowly dying of the drug addict's disease in some group home in Santa Barbara.

After I ushered Kristy and Mrs. Logan out, I loaded up the panel van and went down to the local forensics lab, where Mr. Morris had been transferred. He had been autopsied. I spent the rest of the afternoon carefully piecing his body back together so his young widow and two daughters could see their husband and father at peace. We laid him out in his uniform, and I even managed to coax a small smile onto his face during the embalming. Kristy liked the smile. The service was small because they didn't have many friends here in California. We buried him in Riverside National Cemetery, a fitting setting for one of our country's heroes.

I called Kristy a couple of days after the funeral to follow up. She asked me if it was all right to call me periodically—at work, of course—just to talk to someone. I offered to refer her to a grief counselor. She declined, saying she just needed another grown-up to have a normal conversation with from time to time. I gave her my cell phone number and told her to call me any time she needed to talk.

And thus, our friendship started.

She, the newly widowed, lonely orphan and I, the young undertaker ten years her junior who had recently buried her citizen-soldier husband, became fast friends. We talked nearly every other day and began to "instant message" over the course of many an evening. What started as pity, on my part, blossomed into one of the most beautiful and fulfilling friendships I have ever experienced.

Our casual chats turned into morning coffee at a local café that turned into casual lunches that turned into barbeques over at Kristy's house on lazy Sunday afternoons. I got to meet her two beautiful daughters, Cindy and Jacqueline, and took my "child," Chloe, over too. The girls loved Chloe and fussed over her like she was their baby. Chloe loved the attention the girls bestowed upon her and would grow very excited when I loaded her in the car because she knew she was going to the Morris house.

I gave the girls rides on my bike around their neighborhood and began taking Kristy for long rides out into the Mojave. We both loved the loud silence and solitude a motorcycle can offer, the desert scenery whipping by. I think initially Kristy might have harbored some romantic feelings for me, but I made sure to steer well clear of anything of a suggestive nature. I didn't want to complicate our beautiful friendship. The two orphans had found each other and now felt complete and whole. It was as simple as that. We were each other's missing family.

I had the first Christmas I could remember that I looked forward to. It was the first time in my six years at the mortuary that I didn't volunteer to work so others could be with their families on Christmas Day.

Then, six months after meeting Kristy, I got a call from Mrs. Logan.

Kristy had been killed in a car accident.

Just as suddenly as Kristy had appeared in my life, she left. I drove down to the forensics lab and picked up what remained of her body and gave her the last gift I had to give; I embalmed her.

Kristy's was the only funeral I have ever cried at. I shed not a tear as my father's casket was lowered into the ground or when my grandmother's frail form lay in the front of the chapel. But I sat between Jacqueline and Cindy in the nearly empty chapel as the minister proffered his words and bawled harder than I can ever remember. Chloe sat crouched on the floor at the feet of the three orphans, her ears flat against her head. When we lowered Kristy's simple wooden casket into the ground above her husband's, I felt as though a piece of me was being buried in that hole.

The next day, I unloaded Chloe on my neighbor for a few days, called out of work, and took my Soft Tail out on the road. I wasn't sure where I was headed, but I ended up at Death Valley National Park. The barren vista spread out before my bike as it ate up the open road as fast as I could push it. I could almost feel Kristy's arms wrapped around my body, holding on.

Jacqueline and Cindy are now 18 and 16, having been taken in and raised by Mrs. Logan and her husband. I still take Chloe over to visit, and even though her muzzle is gray and she is a little stiff, she still jumps around a little when I open the car door. She loves those girls almost as much as I do.

CHAPTER 43

Date Destination: "The Morgue"

Contributed by a paintballer

hen I served my apprenticeship I lived in an apartment on the second floor of the funeral home, a big old mansion that had been converted to its current purpose. The owner's family used to live on the second floor, but they had long since moved out and the space had been turned into arrangement offices and the casket selection room—and, of course, my little dungeon room, referred to by the owner as the apprentice's apartment.

My "apartment" was twelve feet square with a tiny bathroom and kitchenette. I didn't care in the least that it was small, in fact, I loved it. It was like having my own place. I had the walls plastered with rock 'n' roll posters. My giant stereo system, set up on cinderblocks and plank shelving, dominated one wall and I had the place all decked out with tapestries, black lights, lava lamps, and the like. It was truly a bachelor's paradise.

In return for living for free at the funeral home, I had to work all the wakes and answer the business phone on weeknights. On Saturday and Sunday nights the owner of the funeral home answered the business phone to give me a couple of nights off. I looked forward to those nights, when I could go out carousing.

I was single and liked to party. Contrary to most people's perception of funeral directors, some of us do let our hair down on occasion.

Unfortunately, my living situation sometimes hindered my luck with the fairer sex. I could never bring girls back to my place; they'd think I was a total creep. Whenever I met a girl out at a bar or club, I'd always talk her into going back to her place. It's kind of hard to get a girl in the mood when she's scared of a dead person popping out of every corner. To me, there is nothing even remotely spooky about a funeral home, but I'm sure to the average person (let alone a drunk female), a funeral home can be a very creepy place. So, to use a baseball metaphor, I always liked to play on the away field. That is, until the night I met the girl of my dreams, and the situation forced me to use the home field advantage.

What a disaster.

It was a Saturday. I had to work late into the evening. By the time I escaped the funeral home and managed to get to Cues, one of my favorite haunts, my friends were already a couple of pitchers deep. Cues is a dark, smoky little dive at the edge of the city whose only redeeming value is that it has the perpetual special of free pool and two dollar pitchers of Pabst Blue Ribbon.

After I lost a goodly amount of money at pool, my group migrated over to a brewpub for steaks and micro-brews. We were eating and drinking and having a good time. Next thing I knew, it was last call. We all ordered one more round before I piled as many as could fit into my Honda. The rest were left to hail a taxi. I had *no* business driving, but times were different then and somehow I managed to get us to a late-night club called Rewind. There is nothing particularly great about Rewind. It's just your basic club: loud music, overpriced drinks, crazy lights, and loose women. The main reason we always went there is that I knew the bouncer and he let us bypass the line.

The club was just filling up when we arrived. The ubiquitous techno music blared, and the emcee was inviting girls up to dance on the giant clear Lucite blocks on stage. I located my favorite bartender and ordered the usual, Knob Creek, neat. I stood and chatted with some of my friends at a high-top table for an hour or so, throwing back a couple more bourbons until the club had filled up and it was just one big sweaty, throbbing, throng of people. I went out and danced for a bit and did my thing.

After I got the cold shoulder from three chicks, I decided it was time to go. I was drunk, and obviously going to be unlucky on this weekend. I sidled up to the bar next to a raven-haired beauty for one more drink. The girl was gorgeous, and had legs that went on forever up into her black mini-skirt.

"Can I buy you a drink, sweetheart?" I asked, offhandedly, expecting her to tell me what I could do with myself.

"Sure," she replied perkily. She smiled, exposing a mouth full of even white teeth, dimples lining her cheeks. "Whatcha drinking?"

"A double Knob Creek, neat."

"I'll have what he's having," she called to the bartender, holding two fingers up. Then she turned to me and smiled slyly. "What's the occasion?" Her crystal blue eyes sparkled with mischief.

I was speechless, and a little stupid from too much booze. "Uh, no occasion," was all I could think of.

The drinks came, and the girl knocked her double bourbon back in one gulp, wiped her mouth with the back of her hand, and said, "C'mon, let's go dance."

I had no choice but to gulp mine down as she grabbed my hand and dragged me out onto the dance floor. As the wee hours of the morning progressed, and the drinks kept flowing, the dancing got more risqué. I'm not a great dancer by any stretch of the imagination, but this girl made me feel like a rock star. By the end of the night when the club lights went up, my head was swimming and I was in the middle of the dance floor making out with the gorgeous girl, whose name I learned was Paula.

"Let's get out of here," she panted.

"Good idea," I agreed. In fact, I couldn't think of a better idea. I was really digging Paula.

We ran out onto the curb before the mobs made their exodus and I hailed one of the taxis waiting in the queue. "Where to?" I asked. "Your place?"

"No, yours," she said.

"I don't want to go there. My place is just a small crappy apartment. Let's go to yours," I urged.

"We can't," she said. "I live at home with my parents. I'm on break from Ohio State. They aren't cool with this." She made a little turning motion with her index finger. "So, it's your place or none." To accentuate her point she put her hand on my thigh.

I froze. I didn't know what to do. I sat there for a few moments.

"Well?" Paula asked. She massaged my thigh harder, imploring me with her blue eyes.

I knew what I had to do.

"Okay," I grudgingly agreed. "My place." I gave the taxi driver the address and off we went.

We made out the whole ride to the funeral home, our hands exploring. The ride was a blur. I remember her raven hair shrouding my face and the spicy smell of her perfume. The next thing I knew, the driver had the dome light on and was demanding his money.

We piled out and Paula exclaimed, "You told me you had a tiny apartment. Look at this place! It's huge! You live alone?"

"Yeah," I replied. "I live alone." She obviously was too intoxicated to notice the giant sign that read "Funeral Home" and I didn't point it out to her. I was too excited at the prospect of what was going to happen once we got up to the apartment to want to ruin it. I had been sampling the goods in the taxi, and I liked what I had sampled thus far. Paula was sumptuous.

I fumbled with the lock on the back door and led her down the hallway to the back staircase that led up to my apartment.

"You have a real nice place," Paula commented, looking at the artwork on the wall in the darkened hallway. "I love how you've decorated it."

"Yeah, yeah," I said distractedly as I opened the door that hid the back staircase as well as the door to the preparation room, "real nice, isn't it?" I wanted to get her upstairs as quickly as possible and continue what we had started in the taxi.

Behind me, Paula let out a blood-curdling scream. "What the fuck?" she screamed. "I'm in a morgue! Oh God, I'm in a morgue!" She took off down the hallway, banging off the walls like a pinball.

I saw someone had left the preparation room door propped open. *Shit!*

"Paula, wait!" I called and took off after her.

She hit the crash bar to the back door and it swung open. She ran into the middle of the front yard and staggered around in small circles like a punch drunk boxer.

"Settle down, Paula. Come on back in," I called from the back door. "It's a funeral home. Not a morgue—"

"I saw a sign that said morgue!"

"Yeah, a sign on the preparation room door. We're not going in there; we're going upstairs to where I live."

"You brought me to a morgue!" she screamed.

I tried to quiet her down.

She was having none of it. "You live at the morgue!"

"I work here. It's okay. I promise." I beckoned with my hand. "Come on. It's safe."

"I don't care!" she cried. "You brought me to a place where there's dead people, you psycho!"

"Keep your voice down," I hissed, looking around at the neighboring houses. It was just starting to get light out and I didn't want to cause a scene on the front lawn of the funeral home. "People live around here."

"I don't give a shit, psycho! There is no way in hell I'm going back in that morgue."

"It's not a—"

"I need a ride home!" she demanded.

"Look, Paula," I pleaded. "We came in a taxi. I have no way to drive you home." My mind momentarily flashed to the hearse in the garage, but immediately nixed the idea. "My car is in the city," I continued. "Just come in and we'll go right to my apartment. There are no dead people up there. It's safe." I saw my chances of romance slipping away before my eyes and there was not a damn thing I could do about it.

Paula stood there swaying in the front yard of the funeral home, under the big elm tree, her eyes half-lidded and clouded over with hatred. "I'll walk then. I'm not stepping foot in that morgue."

She set off unsteadily down the road. "Wait," I called after her. "Do you even know where you're going?"

She threw up her middle finger over her shoulder as she marched down the road. I stood at the back door, slightly bewildered, and watched her go.

CHAPTER 44

Gobble Gobble

Contributed by a vintage LP collector

I made settlement on my dream house on the Monday be-fore turkey day. It's a Cape-style house with all the ameni-ties: random plank hardwood floors, stainless appliances and frameless cabinets in the kitchen, and copious amounts of marble in the bathrooms. My new digs are certainly a step up from my starter house on the West End and certainly a far cry from the fleabag apartment I used to rent in downtown Rich-mond when I first got my license. It's in the kind of neighbor-hood where you'd expect June and Ward Cleaver to exit the house next door at any minute and welcome you to the neighborhood with a fruit basket and bottle of bubbly. I had been saving for this house since...forever.

Naturally, eager to showcase my new bastion, I insisted to my family that I would host Thanksgiving dinner that year. Many of them had already made plans, but I begged, pleaded, cajoled, and threatened, and eventually got my way. It was settled. Word cir-culated throughout the family; Thanksgiving was going to be at Amy's new house. I was thrilled.

I pushed all the boxes into the basement, tidied up as best as possible, bought a Martha Stewart cookbook (my first cookbook ever), and set out to work in the kitchen. It was only a minor disaster, seeing as how my sister, who was little Miss Easy-Bake Oven when we were kids, came over and saved my ass—and my turkey's. The dinner was a smashing success second only to the glory of my new house. The booze flowed—though not for my boyfriend and me who were working—and I gave tours of the house while my pup, Izzy, raced around her new yard. Right before dessert, I received a knock at the door.

I opened the door and greeted a woman who held an extremely large covered roasting pan. Her dazzling smile suggested thousands of dollars of orthodontic work and many whitening treatments.

"Hi. My name is"—I'm not kidding you—"June. I'm your new next door neighbor." She nodded her head perkily as in affirmation of her own name. Not a single stand of hair in her perfect hairstyle moved.

Did you bring Wally and the Beav? I thought derisively, but instead held out my hand and said, "Hi! Nice to meet you," Then, realizing June's hands were full, I withdrew it quickly, feeling foolish. "I'm Amy. Would you care to come in?" I stepped aside and motioned her in.

"Oh no, dear, I'm just so sorry to meet you under these circumstances, but I thought this would help...on behalf of the entire neighborhood."

I was puzzled. *Help?* But I took the pan from her hands. It was so heavy that I had to set it down on a side table to peek under the foil. It was a giant roasted turkey. Seeing the look on my face, June chimed in, "Twenty-five pounds, dear."

I hated it when people called me "dear." I straightened up, cocked my head, and said, "Well, thank you, June. You didn't have to do that. It's awfully extravagant, a whole big turkey."

"I know, but I had an extra one in the freezer and I thought you wouldn't feel like cooking one. So I'm just glad I can give you some semblance of a Thanksgiving Day."

"How do you mean?" I asked, now clearly lost.

"It's always tough when a family member dies. I know. I lost my father two years ago." She reached out, took my hand, and made a hand sandwich.

"Nobody died," I said slowly as understanding began to dawn on me.

"The hearse—"

I cut in, beginning to laugh. "I'm a funeral director."

"But the cop car, the medical examiner's truck," she stalled, and her perky manner fizzled into bewilderment.

"My boyfriend is a county cop. We're both working today, so I have the hearse in case I get called out and my boyfriend is 'code seven,' or on a meal break, right now. My good friend works for the Central District Division of Forensic Science, and like me, is on call today, which is why the Department of Forensic Science truck is here."

June looked absolutely deflated. The battle story she had been planning to tell the garden club had been ruined! I put an arm around her. "Come on in for a drink. You look like you could use one," I teased.

She shook her head. "No. I have to get back to my family," she said. "But I guess it's good nobody died." The white smile was back, this time fake.

"Yeah," I agreed. "Means I can have a peaceful meal with my family."

June's smile tightened in her face of foundation and lipstick.

"You'll get used to seeing the hearse. I bring it home every night I'm taking death call and unfortunately, it won't fit in the garage."

"Oh," June said in a tone that made it clear she abhorred the idea of a death mobile parked next to her house.

"Want your turkey back?"

"No. Consider it a welcome-to-the-neighborhood gift, and Happy Thanksgiving."

"Gobble gobble to you too!" I called after her.

Chuckling, I walked into the dining room holding the covered pan and announced, "Guess what's for dessert?"

CHAPTER 45

The Tapestry of Life

Contributed by a homemaker

M y husband is a funeral director in a small town. We're pretty much the only game in town. Everybody knows us and we know everybody. When I first moved to here it was suffocating. I grew up in the city—where I met Anthony while he was attending mortuary school—and thrived in the cosmopolitan atmosphere. Here, the only thing open after six o'clock is the billiards hall if you're game for a pitcher of cheap beer. But I've grown to love the small-town atmosphere. This is my home now.

I often help out at the funeral home. I usually go over for a couple of hours a day and do the bookkeeping and help clean the place up. Since I don't work, other than volunteering at the elementary school library, I don't mind lending a hand. Sometimes I'll even greet people at the door; it's the type of town where I can almost greet everyone who walks through the door by name.

My husband and I have two children, a boy and a girl, who are exactly a year apart. Kelli is a senior and Trevor is a junior in high school. Four years ago, when the kids were in middle school, I had my first dose of providing service to a loved one when we got that middle-of-the-night call from an Indiana State Patrolman. I guess I always viewed Anthony's profession as serving the families of little old ladies and stately old gentlemen of the community. Clean death. Timely death. Theoretical death. Anthony is a little more steeled in dealing with death, but for me, the experience was all at once confusing and devastating. But even in the shadow of death, I ended up learning a lot about life.

It all began with the dreadful call.

It wasn't unusual to receive middle-of-the-night phone calls, and it wasn't until my husband sat up and exclaimed, "Oh, my God! Where? When?," that I knew something was terribly wrong. Anthony scribbled something on a scrap of paper and said, "Thank you, officer. Please pass along to the family that we'll be there as quickly as we can."

"What's wrong?" I asked. There was a knot in my stomach, though I didn't know why.

"Marie," he said. His face was white. "There's been a terrible accident. Jim and little Jimmy are dead. Grace and Phoebe are in intensive care."

I felt like I had been punched in the gut. Jim and Grace Brewer are close friends of ours. Jim and Anthony had been friends in high school and when Grace and Jim had started going together shortly after Anthony and I married, we had double-dated a lot. Their son and daughter were exactly our son and daughter's ages and they went to school together.

"How?" I managed to get out.

Anthony put his glasses on, got out of bed, and clicked the light on. "On their way back from Jim's parents in Chicago, they got into a car wreck. That's all I know right now." His voice was unusually tight. "Get your clothes on. I'll call my mom and see if she can come over and watch the kids."

"Me?"

"Yeah, you're going."

"What? Why?" I was confused, and scared.

"Your friend's husband is dead and she's laying in a hospital somewhere. She needs *you*. We've got to go take care of our friends."

I got out of bed and mechanically put my clothes on. I felt like Tom Hanks in the movie *Saving Private Ryan* when he landed on Omaha Beach on D-Day; sounds were muted and everything moved in slow motion. It took me forever to put my clothes on and brush my hair back into a ponytail. By the time I got downstairs Anthony had every light in the house blazing and was gone.

I sat at the kitchen counter. Anthony and his mother and father pulled up simultaneously, Anthony in the hearse, and his parents in their Buick. "Hi Mom. Hi Dad," I said automatically as they trooped in. Anthony's dad was still in his pajamas and his mom in her nightie. They had obviously been roused from a deep sleep.

His mother rushed over and gave me a giant hug. "Oh, Marie!" she said. "We're so sorry. Jim was such a nice boy!"

"You okay here?" Anthony asked his parents. He was all business.

"Of course, Tony!" his mother said. "Go, go."

"Get the kids up and off to school. Bus comes at ten of seven."

"Where should we tell them you've gone?" his mother asked.

"I don't know, Mom," he said. He sounded tired all of a sudden. "Make something up. Marie and I will tell them about the Brewers when we get back. No sense you having to do that."

We said goodbye and Anthony and I got in the hearse.

"Where are we going?" I asked.

"Looks like it's going to be a four or five hour ride from here. Hopefully, traffic won't be that bad this time of night."

I looked at the clock. It read 11:49.

"How are you going to get two bodies into the back of this thing?" I asked, craning around to peer through the little window partition separating the cabin from the bed of the hearse. It looked like there was only one cot in the back.

"Reeves cot."

"Huh?"

"It's a collapsible cot that folds up. Like a reinforced yoga mat, I guess."

"Oh."

"I'll put the boy on that. They'll both fit."

I noticed how he didn't call Jimmy by name, but "the boy."

"Okay," I said, still numb.

As we drove up through Kentucky, Anthony and I were both silent. I wracked my brain for something to say to Grace. Anything. I couldn't think of any words of encouragement or sympathy that fit this situation. *Her husband and child were dead! Dead.* For the longest time I just sat in silence, thinking, but *not* thinking. The tension built in me as I searched and nothing came. Finally, I couldn't stand it any longer and blurted out, "What am I supposed to say to her, Ant?"

He kept his eyes glued to the road. "What can you say? Say something from the heart." He fell silent again.

"What are you going to say?" I asked him. My words issued like gunshots in a library.

"Dunno." He pushed his glasses up on his nose and cleared his throat. "I'll think of something, I imagine."

I shut my mouth. The silence descended back over the hearse. When we passed from Kentucky into Indiana, Anthony and I had not broken the silence and I was still drawing a blank. There was nothing I could say. We passed Indianapolis in silence and still I could think of *nothing* to say to my friend.

Anthony consulted a map stored in the door pocket a couple of times and a scrap of paper several times over the course of the next hour before we pulled under the portico of the hospital.

"Here we are," Anthony announced. "I'll go check things out. Wait here."

The interior light of the hearse flicked on and then off; I was left again in darkness.

I was alone with my empty mind. The hot engine ticked loudly. I began to panic. We had driven over five hours and I hadn't thought of a single thing to say! I hoped I would be spurred into some deep thought or philosophy to share with Grace, but the panic just compounded my mental block. I could think of nothing but my friend and her little girl lying upstairs with tubes and monitors attached to their broken bodies while her husband and son lay on slabs in the morgue. I shivered and clenched my fingers so hard in my palms I drew blood.

So engrossed was I in my thoughts that when Anthony swung the hearse door open, I jumped.

"Marie, everything all right?" he asked.

He had a concerned look on his face, but I could tell his mind was elsewhere.

"Sure. Fine," I said quickly.

"Okay. Why don't you go on in." It was a command not a question. "The lady at the reception desk will tell you where to go. I've already told her our situation. It's not normal visiting hours, but she'll let you go up. I have to take the hearse around back and park it. This will save you from having to trudge through the basement."

I nodded and got out of the hearse. Anthony dropped it in gear and roared away. I put my arms around myself and walked through the front door of the hospital.

It was worse than I thought it would be. Grace lay propped up in bed with tubes and wires covering every inch of her body. I couldn't imagine a human was under all the bandages and dressings. Her head was half covered by a giant bandage. The gauze had a giant brown spot of dried blood on it.

The room held the pungent smell of hospitals: powerful disinfectants and fear. Grace's room was dark save the glow of the monitors. One of the machines gave off a constant *beep beep* sound. The sound, marking the passing time, was maddening.

To my relief, Grace was asleep. I dragged a chair next to her bed and laid my hand upon her tube-covered hand. She stirred. I'm not sure if she could see me as her face was so swollen, but she could certainly sense me. She tried forming words around the tube going down her throat.

I swallowed and tried to speak, offer my sympathies, *something*, but my words sounded clumsy so I just finished with, "Anthony and I are here for you and Phoebe. Just rest. We're here for you." I made quiet shushing sounds and just stroked her hand until she seemed to drift off again.

After a bit, Anthony strolled into the room. "How is she?"

"She knows we're here." I looked at him. "That's all that matters."

"I stopped and checked on Phoebe. The nurse told me her prognosis is much better than her mother's."

"That's good," I replied. It didn't feel like it was me speaking the words. I felt so disconnected.

We stayed for a couple more hours until it was time for Grace's first scheduled surgery of the day. Anthony loaded Jim and Jim, Jr., into the hearse and we began the long trek back to Tennessee. The return ride was just as silent as the previous one. When we got home, Anthony went right to the funeral home to perform his work and I crashed in bed. I woke hours later, still tired, and made my way down to the kitchen, where I found Anthony.

"Ant?"

He gave me a look of pure exhaustion. Anthony was used to late nights, but I had never seen him this tired before.

I massaged his shoulders. "How was it?" I asked.

"Tough."

"Want to talk about it?" I wrapped my arms around him. The sweet smell of formaldehyde lingered on his shirt.

"No."

He was silent. I knew it had been hard on him. His employee, Violet, had called to say she had found him crying in the garage in his embalming suit. I knew Anthony was too tough to ever admit it to me. I'd press the issue at a later time; give him a little space for now.

"Ant," I said tentatively.

"Yeah?"

"I think I need to go back—to the hospital."

"Really? Don't you think Jim's parents will drive down? And obviously Grace's will fly out to be with them."

"I'm sure they will." I paused. "I just need to go be with her."

"How long are you going to go?" he asked.

"However long it takes."

"And the kids?"

"We'll tell them before I go. Then you can get some sleep. I'll ask your mom and dad to come over and sit this evening."

"Okay," he said. I could tell he was too tired to even function.

"Kids—" I called.

I sat next to Grace's bed. She wore a number of casts, and the bandage on her head was fresh. The head nurse assured me the surgeries had been as successful as one could hope, and they were guardedly optimistic about her recovery.

The tube had been removed from Grace's throat, and when she woke she tried talking. Some of the swelling on her face had subsided, but she would definitely need an oral surgeon sometime in the very near future. Her voice came out in raspy whispers. "Did Ant take care of Jim and little Jimmy?" she asked, tears rolling down her face.

I nodded, tears running down my face, too. I couldn't speak.

Grace tried speaking again, but I interrupted her, "Grace, don't talk. Please. Just rest." I squeezed her hand.

"You know, Marie," she said, ignoring my protest. I had to strain to make out the words. "I sometimes think life is like a tapestry. And—" She stopped and winced as her tongue traced over broken teeth. "And...we're looking at the back. We're looking at the mess of tangled threads—knots and threads going every which way. It's seemingly meaningless."

Tears flowed freely down my cheeks, and I held my friend's

hand tightly as she continued, "Walk around that same tangled mess and on the other side is a breathtaking piece of art. I think— I think we only get to look at the back of the tapestry most of the time. Right now, I'm only seeing chaos and knots and loose threads. I know though, *I know,* that one day I'll get to look at the front and it'll all make sense. It'll all make so much sense…I'll get to see the beauty of God's work.

"Thank Ant for me. He bore his cross."

CHAPTER 46

The Gay Man in the Wine Bottle

Contributed by a vintner

M y partner and I met Charles and Jacques when we were touring the Bordeaux wine region for the first time. We ran into these Americans at an outdoor café, started talking, and found out that not only were they from the same state, but they lived about ten minutes from Wes's and my house. They live in Concord and we live just north of Manchester. We exchanged numbers and have since become good friends and travel buddies.

I am a funeral director and Wes is a general surgeon at one of the local hospitals. In between our hectic schedules we don't have as much time together as we'd like, but we make time for our shared hobby, making wine. We've been making wines for over twenty years now and have gotten to a point where we can turn out a pretty good bottle of *vin*. We make all sorts of whites and reds, depending on what's in season when we're making a batch. Our friends rave that our wines are better than store-bought, but mostly I think they're blowing smoke.

Since Wes and I are wine freaks, we naturally like to tour wine regions when we go on vacation. After we became friends with Charles and Jacques, they started tagging along on our wine touring extravaganzas, not necessarily for the winery tours, but for the destinations. Wes and I would go and do our wine thing and they'd go off on their own sightseeing thing. We'd been traveling together for fifteen years with destinations including Melbourne, Napa, Sonoma, Bilbaon Rioja, and Mendoza, to name a few.

Charles came to me one day and asked me to handle his funeral arrangements. He had HIV. This was before the antiretroviral drug cocktails; the disease had progressed to such a point that the available drugs could only prolong his life. He lasted four years, six months, and nine days.

Charles had moved from his home state of Louisiana the day he turned eighteen. He needed to be somewhere a little more liberal than the Deep South, and he ended up in Massachusetts. As soon as Charles's family found out about his "affliction," they disowned him. Charles hadn't spoken to his family since. When his father died in the mid '80s, Charles received a letter in the mail, months after the fact, from an aunt telling him what had happened. She told him not to send his sympathies to his mother.

The day Charles came into the funeral home to make arrangements for himself, he told me, "I want to be cremated and my ashes to go to Jacques," who, at the time, had been his companion for seventeen years. "I am going to extend the same courtesy to my family that they extended to me when daddy died."

He handed me a sealed envelope addressed to his aunt.

"Promise me you'll mail it *after*—" He choked off the rest of the sentence.

I nodded and patted him on the back.

"She'll tell my mother and even though I haven't spoken to that woman in twenty-nine years, I know she is going to come north, playing the mother card, and demand my ashes," he cautioned me. "Curt, under no circumstances are you to give them to her. I have made Jacques the executor of my estate; the beneficiary of every earthly possession I have, and have had my lawyer draw up an affidavit that says Jacques gets my remains. Promise me you'll give them to him."

I promised him.

With a twinkle in his eye, he added, "I've also done a lot of thinking—this disease makes you do that—about my urn. Will you bottle me?"

"Huh?" I replied, shocked.

"You know, put me in one of your wine bottles and cork me. I figured since I like to drink wine, and I like to drink *your* wine, it'll be perfect. Besides, it looks less threatening than," he did air quotes with his fingers, "an urn." He rolled his eyes in the fashion that only women and gays can.

I laughed, but Charles assured me he was serious.

"All right," I acquiesced. "I'll bottle you. You want a label?"

"Nah, just cork me."

That conversation was the beginning of the end.

Wes did all he could for him over the four years, but at the time our knowledge of HIV wasn't what it is now, and Charles withered and died.

On the day of his death, Wes's care stopped and mine started. I fulfilled Charles's wish and cremated his earthly remains. I also dropped the letter to his aunt in the mail.

Two weeks passed. I finally found it within me to take one of the empty glass wine bottles and the corker to the funeral home. Human cremains can range in color from white to gray to even a pinkish color. Charles's were gray. I ran a magnet over the cremains to pick up any metal fragments and then ran them through the processor that crushes any big bone chips and turns them into the type of "ashes" the general public would be familiar with, fireplace-looking ashes.

I put the bottle under the funnel of the transfer machine and poured the ash from the transfer can until the wine bottle was full, setting aside the small amount left over for myself. I was going to scatter them next time I was in Napa, Charles's favorite wine region. I corked the green glass bottle and set it on a shelf in my office.

Charles sat on my shelf for at least another week while Jacques summoned the courage to come pick up his former partner. It was during this time that I was sitting at the reception desk in the lobby, breaking the receptionist for lunch, when a pleasant-looking elderly woman walked in. The woman, who was quite plump, was dressed neatly in a light pink, old-lady-type pantsuit. She strolled up to the reception desk.

"Hello," she said in a Southern drawl.

I curiously stared at her big hair, but only for a moment. "Can I help you?"

"I'm Constance de Baptiste."

I raised my eyebrows. "Okay."

"I'm here to take my Charles back to the family plot in L'isiana."

I paused, stunned, and my heart stopped beating as Jacques walked in the front door behind her, but I recovered enough to say to Charles's mother, "Okay, ma'am. Why don't you take a seat over there and I can help you in five minutes. A gentleman who has an appointment to pick something up has just arrived. It shouldn't take long."

"That will be just fine, young man," she said.

Charles's words echoed through my head, *Curt, under no circumstances are you to give them to her,* as Jacques walked up to the counter, and for a moment Mrs. de Baptiste and her son's lover were side by side, though neither knew it. Charles didn't keep any pictures of his family around, so Jacques couldn't know what she looked like, and Mrs. de Baptiste had no idea what her son's lover of almost twenty-two years looked like. They glanced at each other the way strangers do, then Mrs. de Baptiste walked across the lobby and plunked all of herself down in one of our couches and opened a magazine.

I held my hand in such a way that my pointing finger was shielded from Mrs. de Baptiste as I pointed to her and mouthed

Charles's mother. Jacques's eyes got real wide and his mouth dropped open in an "Oh, my gosh" expression.

"Could I get you something to drink while you wait, ma'am?" I called over Jacques' shoulder.

"Dear no," she replied. "I won't even be that long. But thank you."

She went back to her magazine and I hunched over the counter so Jacques and I could talk in conspiratorial tones.

"That's really her?" he asked. "No joke?"

"Seriously. It's Charles's mom."

"I expected some hillbilly with no teeth wearing overalls!" Jacques exclaimed.

"Shhh! She'll hear you, but yes, she is quite unlike what I pictured. And she speaks like she's very well educated."

"I never would have thought it," Jacques said, shaking his head. "Charles always made them sound like they were backwoods type people."

"Just backwards thinking people," I said.

Jaques repeated, "I never would have thought it."

"Me neither," I said, putting my hand on top of his in a friendly way. "That aside. How are you doing?"

"Hanging in there ... I guess. I miss him a lot, especially at night when I'm alone. He was such a large presence. There's nothing now."

"Wes and I are here for you. You know that."

"I know."

"Let me go get him. I've got him all bottled up for you." I disappeared into the back and returned with the bottle, which I handed to Jacques with great fanfare, and said loudly enough that Mrs. de Baptiste could hear, "Here's a bottle of the finest. The finest I've ever known for sure."

"Thank you, Curt," he said with tears in his eyes that he quickly dashed.

"Bye," I said quietly.

"Now ma'am," I called to Mrs. de Baptiste. "What did you say I could do for you? I got sidetracked with that gentleman who came to pick up a wine bottle."

Mrs. de Baptiste got up, and as she did, her estranged son came within mere feet of her as Jacques passed her on his way out the door. She looked curiously at the bottle cradled in the man's arms; its contents hidden by opaque green glass.

She trundled over to the counter. "A bottle of wine?" Her Southern drawl made her sound as though she was talking with a mouth full of syrup.

"Yes. A little unusual, but I make wine in my spare time, and sometimes my patrons will ask for a bottle."

"Isn't that marvelous," she said as if she wasn't sure if it was or not. "But I have no time to be drinking wine at a funeral parlor." Parlor sounded like par-luh. "I have come for my Charles and then I have a flight to catch back to L'isiana."

"Your Charles? I'm sorry, ma'am, but his cremains are no longer here," I said truthfully. The door closed behind Jacques. "His partner came to pick him up already. That's what Charles wanted; I have a signed affidavit allowing me to release his cremains to his partner if you would like to see that document."

The Southern belle façade cracked.

She spluttered. She threatened. She menaced.

I stood staunch and collected.

In the end, she flew back to Louisiana without her dear Charles, but what matters is that Charles is where he should be, where *he* wanted to be.

CHAPTER 47

The First Date

Contributed by a writer

M y parents had been away on vacation to the Cajun capital—New Orleans—and I was meeting them to eat when their flight landed. It was summertime, and, as usual, thunderstorms had delayed their flight. I was already at the restaurant when they called me from the tarmac. It was a nice night so I got myself a drink from the bar and decided to wait outside. I ran into an old friend and his girlfriend outside. We reminisced for a few minutes before they went in to eat, and I gave him my phone number. We'd catch up, I told him.

I ordered another drink, my parents arrived soon, and I promptly forgot about the encounter.

A couple of weeks later I was at my parents' beach house and received a call from the old friend. His girlfriend's parents had rented a house the next town over, and would I be interested in going out to the bar? *Would I? Does the Pontiff live in Rome? Of course I would!* I spent the night out at the bar with him, his girlfriend, her sister, and a couple of other people. We had a great time. The next morning I had a raging headache, but I had the sister's phone number and thus ended my weekend at the beach.

That Monday began my week on call—the week when I had

to take night calls and go out on death removals. I generally don't like to get involved in things I can't be readily torn away from when I'm on call, but I didn't want to wait another week before I could take the sister out on a date. I decided to set up a date. *What are the chances I'll get a death call during a two-hour dinner?* I rationalized.

So, I called Melissa and asked her out to dinner.

She accepted.

At the time of our proposed first date, Melissa happened to be working at a pharmacy right across the highway from the funeral home. Naturally, I suggested a restaurant that shared the same parking lot with the pharmacy for convenience's sake. I also made the verbal disclaimer that I would be on call that night, and might have to leave. She seemed fine with that. We agreed to meet when she got off work at eight o'clock.

I met Melissa at the restaurant and we were seated immediately. Due to the lateness of the hour, the place was fairly empty and the service was fast. The waiter came up and asked for our drink orders.

"I'll have a margarita," she said.

"Club soda with lemon," I said. The waiter left. Melissa looked at me strangely, as if to ask, *Why didn't you order a drink also?* "I don't drink," I said, deadpan.

"But you were drinking last weekend—" she said, obviously confused.

I laughed. "I know. Just kidding. I don't drink when I'm working."

"Oh." She nodded like she understood, but still had a puzzled look on her face.

We sipped our drinks, talked, and ordered our food. I was really enjoying her company. It's quite different to talk to someone one-on-one in a quiet setting, sober, than yelling over the din of a packed beach bar at each other, totally smashed. I was glad I had gotten her number. Our food came and about five seconds later my pager buzzed.

"Excuse me," I said and whipped out my phone.

I called the familiar number. Someone was dead. I had to go on the removal.

"Listen," I said, signaling to the waiter, "I have to go."

The waiter trotted over. "I need the check please. ASAP," I said to him, handing him my credit card. He scurried off.

"I need to go on a removal. Sorry to cut the date short—" I signed the check that the waiter thrust in my face. "But I'll call you later when I get home."

I hopped up, leaving Melissa sitting alone in the booth with two piping hot entrees and a baffled look on her face.

She later told me that when she arrived home at eight thirty, looking confused, her father said to her, "You know, there are services out there that a guy can hire to call him so that he can abort the date if it's going bad."

Apparently, when I had told her I had to "work" that night she didn't know what I was talking about because she didn't know my profession. But since then she's gotten used to my having to drop everything and go to work. For some reason, the first date wasn't bad enough not to say "yes" fifteen months later. We're now happily married and love recounting the tale of our inglorious first date.

In fact, we ran the story of our first date along with the announcement of our wedding in our local paper.

CHAPTER 48

Ironic Injustice

Contributed by a woodworker

B uilding a business from the ground up is hard work. Ask anyone who's done it; they'll tell you.

I liken a business to a newborn. At first you have to do everything for it. *Everything*. But as it grows and matures you have to do less and less, until, if you're real smart, you set up a business system where you can just sit back and reap what you've sown.

At the time of this story I hadn't gotten to the reaping point yet; my business was still an infant.

My shingle had only been out for about thirteen months when I had the opportunity to go on my first vacation as business owner. I started with a phone call from Dani. It was a Wednesday. The call went something like this:

"Hey Topher, how's the old swordsman? I haven't talked to you in, like, six months," Dani said.

"Nice to talk to you too, Dani." I tried to put on an air of indignation. "You know that hurts. Really hurts. Just because I like to see what's out there on the dating scene you automatically tag me with those hurtful labels."

"How long did Rachel last?"

"I—"

"How long?" she interrupted.

"Six weeks...but that's not the point!" I huffed.

Dani laughed, airily, the way she always did. "So, seriously, what's going on with you?"

"I'm so stressed!" I groaned.

She laughed again. Dani laughs a lot. "Why's that? No squeeze?"

"No, thank you very much," I replied with mock anger. "I haven't had a day off in thirteen months is why I'm stressed!"

"Stop being so dramatic. I'm sure you're just fine."

"You know that grandfather clock I promised to build for Rob? Just like the one I built for your wedding present?"

"Yeah. What about it?"

"I built the frame thirteen months ago but haven't had the time to do any of the inlay." I paused. "What I'm saying, Dani, is that I haven't done anything but work with dead people for the past year and I need a break."

"That bad?"

"I might as well pitch a tent here in the office."

"Poor you."

"Poor me. I can't even find the time to go do a little speed dating, much less finish a stupid clock."

"Speed dating." She snorted. "Is that what you call it these days?"

"Oh, shut up."

She ignored me as she usually did. I think Dani thought I was too dramatic.

"If you're so stressed then why don't you take a long weekend this upcoming weekend and use my place in the Keys?"

"Are you serious?" I asked.

Dani had a beautiful condo in Lower Matecumbe Key that we used to go to all the time before she had kids. I loved going to her place. It was great for doing nothing and relaxing on the beach, or if you wanted to do something, Key West was just an hour and a half drive down the coastal highway.

"Yeah, sure," Dani said. "Take it. Enjoy yourself. I'll drop the key off at your office tomorrow on my way to the gym."

"Oh my God, Dani, you're a life saver!"

"I wouldn't go that far, but thanks, Toph. One condition though—" she trailed off.

"What would that be, my dear?" I asked coyly. I knew what was coming.

"No strange women in my bed."

"Why Dani, I would never—"

She cut me off. "Save it, lover boy. Gotta run. I'll drop the key tomorrow."

We hung up.

I had met Danielle Brown, or Dani, as her friends call her, about twelve years earlier when I first got into the mortuary business. She worked for the Omega Counseling Center. I was looking for a place to refer clients of mine. We met and became friends.

Dani left Omega to open her own clinic, The Hope Clinic, that specializes in drug and alcohol recovery counseling, something closer to her heart than what she had been doing as a general family counselor at Omega.

Dani found her life's calling after her own bout with alcoholism in her late teens. Her mother and father had both been alcoholics. Her mother died in a drunk driving accident when Dani was ten years old, and her father died of liver cirrhosis about three years ago—I buried him. Now fifteen years sober, Dani is a big advocate for local chapters of AA and MADD programs. Though Dani specializes in addiction counseling, she still takes my referrals as a favor to me; I don't trust my clients with anyone else.

I was embalming a body the morning after our conversation when Dani dropped the keys off with the receptionist, so I didn't get a chance to talk to her. I couldn't wait to get down to Lower

Matecumbe and enjoy some quality time on the beach sipping a
Rum Runner and listening to Ziggy Marley. So excited that I
wasn't even bothered when I was awoken at some god-awful time
the following morning to make a removal.

I hired a trade embalmer to cover for me, gave explicit in-
structions to my apprentice, told my receptionist to hold all my
calls, and headed for the Keys. It's about a six-hour drive from my
mortuary to Lower Matecumbe. I put the top down on my car
and made it to Key Largo in a little less than five hours. Since I
knew Dani's house would be bone-dry, I stopped at a liquor store
for some supplies and then drove another hour down Route 1,
where I made a stop in Islamorada for a couple bags of ice. From
Islamorada, Dani's condo is just a couple of miles. I parked my
Mustang in the palm-shaded lot and left my small gym bag in
the car in favor of unloading the essentials.

I threw open all the windows and immediately set to work pouring Bacardi and Malibu rum over ice in the blender, adding cran-
berry, orange, and pineapple juice, and topping my creation off
with a splash of Bacardi 151 rum. In minutes, I was sitting in a
chair on the beach enjoying my Rum Runner and watching the
sunset. Honestly, watching the sun go down over the gently lap-
ping waves in the Keys is one of the most beautiful things in the
world. All the stress of the past year melted away.

I was about halfway through my cocktail when I felt my phone
vibrate. I cursed and decided not to answer it, but checked the
caller I.D. It was Dani.

Probably just checking to make sure I arrived all right, I thought.
I decided to answer it.

It wasn't Dani. It was Leo, her husband.

"Topher," he said. His voice sounded strange. Strained. "You
need to come back."

"What's wrong?" I asked.

There was a long pause and then he said, "Dani was involved
in a drunk driving accident this evening. She's dead."

My head swam. "But how—"

"She was on her way home from my mother's. She had just dropped the kids off for the weekend—" He gulped. "The driver of the other car hit a guardrail on the freeway and swerved into her. His blood alcohol level was 0.28; he's fine. But Dani—" There was a pause. I thought I had lost the connection. "They said it was instantaneous..." Leo trailed off.

I sat stunned for a moment. I mumbled something into the phone. I heard a garbled, "Thanks," and the line went dead.

With a heavy heart, I retraced my steps north to give Dani the last gift I had to give in our friendship.

The world is filled with injustice, but Dani seemed to have been dealt an especially cruel fate after all she had worked for and achieved. Her death was a bitter pill to swallow. I still kick myself that I didn't come out to say hello to Dani that day she dropped the keys off. I guess what I'm trying to say is: always make your peace with your friends and family because you never know when the last time will be.

CHAPTER 49

Windsor or Prince Albert?

Contributed by a club cricket player

hen I was a boy I had to get dressed up for *everything*. Today, everyone is casual. I see kids in church on Sunday wearing jeans, people in fine dining establishments wearing shorts, and of course, people coming to services at my funeral home in any number of... costumes. I see tee shirts, ripped jeans, sneakers, tawdry mini-skirts, and the like. Gone are the days of dark suited men and elegantly dressed women wearing big hats clustered in the funeral parlor under clouds of blue cigarette smoke, whispering in hushed tones. Casual is in, even at a funeral.

Things sure have changed. For the better, I can't say, but I know when I was a boy my mother insisted I wear a suit for just about every occasion. I can remember wearing a suit on the boardwalk at the shore during family vacations. Can you imagine putting on a suit to go get ice cream? But, growing up as the son of an undertaker, I don't so much remember having to wear my suit for every outing as I do having my father tie my necktie for me.

I would struggle into the starched white shirt with the detachable collar, and then pull on my ill-fitting little dark blue suit. I grew too fast and it always seemed the sleeves were a little too short and the cuffs of the pants a little too high above the tops of my wingtips. Then, tie in hand, I would run to find my father so he could tie it for me.

"What kind of knot are we going to do today, Sport?" he'd ask. "Windsor or Prince Albert?"

"Dad," I'd protest. "Just do the normal!"

"All right, Sport," he'd say, twinkle in his eye. "You know the drill."

I'd lie down on the couch or the floor and he would hover over me, tongue peeking out the side of his mouth as he laboriously swirled the ends of the tie around into the fancy knots my hands could never seem to master. Then, when he was finished, he'd say, "All done, Sport," and I'd hop up and off I'd go, all pressed out in my little suit.

I was so used to this almost daily ritual, that sometimes when I lie on my back, to this day, I expect to see my father's face above mine, the scent of his Old Spice aftershave, his large hands fumbling with my tiny tie.

I could never understand why my mother scolded my father for tying my tie. If she caught my father in the act she would say, "For heaven's sake, stop it, George!" or, "That's terrible, George, it's our son!"

And my father would invariably reply, "What, Mary? It's the only way I know how to do it on someone else! If you don't like it, you do it then."

My mother would then grow silent because she didn't know how to tie a tie, and the issue would be dropped.

It wasn't until later in life that I figured out what my mother was talking about.

My father enlisted in the Army at age 18 and served for three years in a graves registry unit before *the* two bombs were dropped. I can only imagine how horrific his job was as the Allied forces plowed through Europe and he followed in the war machine's gruesome wake. The job, he told me, gave him compassion for the families of the soldiers he bagged and tagged and then buried under French soil. When the war ended, and he was discharged, he opened up a funeral home in his home state and married my mother. I think helping others deal with death must have been his way of coping with the atrocities he saw during the war.

My father confirmed my theory right before his death in a rare candid conversation. My mother had long since died, and my father lay dying of pancreatic cancer in a nursing home. He told me that he couldn't stand the fact that "The only thing I could do was collect their tags and properly identify them while their family was about to see a sedan pull up outside their house somewhere in America."

We talked and reminisced some more. I asked him if he remembered how he used to make me lie down to tie my ties when I was a little boy.

"Yeah, I remember," he replied.

"Could you really not do it unless I was lying down?" I asked him.

"Hell, no!" he had replied. "I can tie my own tie without lying down. I did it just to get a rise out of your mother!"

"So all those years—"

He cut me off. "Yup, all those years I was just giving your mother a hard time."

We both had a good laugh.

I tied a Windsor knot in his necktie less than a week after our conversation.

CHAPTER 50

Thaleia

Contributed by a fisherman

People are insatiably curious about the particulars of the business I work in. I still haven't figured out if it's the mystery surrounding death or the sheer fact that most people are generally ignorant of the basic workings of the business. I get bombarded with all sorts of crazy questions. When I am with a group of people I don't know I've learned to keep my mouth shut when the subject of work comes up because I know the questions that are going to follow. No, the dead do not sit up; no, I have never seen a dead person move, it's impossible; and yes, I am a man who can do makeup. Then the stupid ringer question always follows: "Do you believe in ghosts?"

I hate this question because not only do I feel compelled to answer truthfully, but it opens up a whole other line of questioning. I tell people that not only do I believe in ghosts, but I can prove their existence. This floors them...always.

"How can you prove it?" the offended party then asks.

"Well, for starters, my wife refuses to sleep at home alone—"

Thus begins my dissertation on how I know ghosts exist. It's really simple. Allow me to explain:

My wife and I bought a townhouse in the section of the city that's undergoing an urban renaissance. It's a massive old run down Victorian we spent the better part of six months renovating. In the chaos of working on the house it was hard to detect the paranormal activity, but once we moved in, we realized that our house had come with its very own ghost.

Before I moved into our new house I didn't believe in ghosts; it just wasn't logical. I work in a business where I am around dead people all day. My thought was, once you were dead, that was it, you were dead, end of story. That changed starting with our first night in our new house.

My wife, Sara, and I were awakened sometime in the middle of the night.

"What time is it?" Sara asked.

"I have no idea, our alarm clocks aren't working," I said scratching my head, puzzled.

"Do you hear that?" Sara whispered.

"Yeah, sounds like a party," I said.

And indeed we could hear music downstairs.

"You think it's some sort of surprise?" she asked. "It sounds like there are a lot of people in our house." Sure enough, over the music, the sound of muted laughter, talking, and the clinking of ice in glasses wafted up the stairs.

"Who would have thrown it, especially so late like this?" I fumbled for my watch on the nightstand.

"My parents?" Sara suggested.

I looked at my watch irritably. It read after midnight. "Don't they realize tomorrow is a work day?"

"I don't know. They're random like that."

"Well, let's go check out the party." I sighed and swung the bedroom door open. The light from downstairs filtered up into the upstairs hallway.

Sara put on her robe and followed me.

We went downstairs and found nothing but an empty first floor, all the lights on, and the stereo blaring at near full volume.

I ran over and clicked off the stereo receiver. The silence was deafening.

"You did hear the people, right?" Sara said, standing in the middle of the foyer, looking around, bewildered. I just nodded and began turning off the lights.

"Sonofabitch!" I said when we got upstairs. Our alarm clocks were both glowing their red digits. I fingered the softball bat I had retrieved from the basement, a great sense of unease settling over me.

After that, we were very careful about keeping track of which lights and appliances we turned off. The problem persisted. I wondered if my house experienced weird electrical surges that turned things on. I had an electrician come and look at the wiring. He certified my electrical system to be in perfect working condition and suggested, "Maybe you have a ghost."

I was beginning to think we did. When my car keys started getting hidden, I was sure.

It seemed our ghost had a sense of humor.

My new morning ritual included searching for my car keys. I always hung them on the hook next to the kitchen door when I got home. Every morning they were gone. They were never hard to find. I just had to look a little. Sara, a high school English teacher, nicknamed our ghost Thaleia after the Greek goddess of comedy. She thought it was funny that Thaleia hid my keys. I was glad *she* was amused.

"Wouldn't be so funny if it were happening to you," I grumbled on more than one occasion as I tore through the house, late for work.

In addition to Thaleia's little jokes, like turning on the televisions, getting into bed with us, and the occasional smell of potpourri in different rooms of the house, she liked to play bigger tricks on us. The biggest one I can recall was during the summer after we moved into our house. Sara and I were going on a week-long cruise to Bermuda. The morning before we were set to leave, Sara called to me from the guest bedroom. "Dan, did you move my dress?"

"What dress?" I replied, frantically packing all my stuff last minute, my usual M.O.

"The one I wanted to wear on one of the formal nights," Sara said. "It was white with the big red and black polka dots on it."

"Never seen it." I had no idea what she was talking about.

She strolled into our bedroom, hands on hips. "Well, damn it, Dan, I left it right there hanging on the frame of the closet in the guest room not more than fifteen minutes ago!" She stamped her foot. "You had to have moved it. It didn't just get up and walk off on its own!"

"I'll help you look for it, but I promise, babe, I didn't touch it."

We searched high and low and ended up heading off to catch our flight one dress short.

Upon our return a week later our next-door neighbor, Mr. Williams, greeted us from his usual spot on his front porch—leaning against one of the pillars. He tipped his cabbie hat. "Hi there, Sara." He tipped it again. "Dan. You all coming back from the beach?" He scratched his grizzled face and took a drag of his cigarette. He smoked it out of a holder.

"Nope," Sara chirped, "just coming back from a wonderful trip to Bermuda."

"Huh," Mr. Williams said, and scrunched up his face.

I could tell something didn't sit well with him. He spent a lot of time on his front porch watching the world go by, and was, essentially, the neighborhood watchman.

"How long you been gone?"

"A week," Sara replied.

"Well, someone had one hell of a party in your house two

nights before last. Lots o' carrying on, talkin', laughin' and such…
it went on until all hours. I thought about going over there and
havin' a highball." He laughed a phlegmy, smoker's laugh.

Sara and I looked at each other and exchanged glances. We
knew who had hosted the party.

"Must have been my brother having his friends over for a party
or something," Sara said.

"Or could have been the ghost," I chimed in, joking with Mr.
Williams.

We all laughed, but for different reasons.

"Well, I hope your brother didn't ruin the house too much.
Sounded right wild," Mr. Williams said.

We agreed.

When Sara went upstairs to drop her bags, I heard a scream.
I ran up the steps and found her pointing to her polka dot dress
hanging in the middle of her closet; the other clothes seemed
pushed away from it. "Holy—"

"Take it easy, babe. Maybe Thaleia wanted it for that party she
threw," I said.

"Not funny."

What could we do? We had a ghost. She liked to play with
the electricity and hide things from us, end of story. The incident
with the dress really got me thinking, though. I began to think
about all the people that must have been born and died in the
house over the past 120-plus years and I decided to do a little
research. I went downtown to the local historical society and located the builder for all the homes on the block and then located
the tax records for my house dating back to 1879. On a hunch,
I wrote down all the names of the owners of the house and the
years the property changed hands.

The next day when I went into work, I went down into the
basement where the records are kept and took a look at our funeral service records dating back to 1891, when the company
was founded. They are big, dusty, leather-bound ledgers with one

gilded page dedicated to each entry. Back then, the owner only did fifty calls a year, so I was able to blow through the records pretty quickly. I knew the names I was looking for. It took me a little over an hour and a half to go ten years and find it.

In 1901, the tax records indicated, a man by the name of S. Roemer sold my house. The 1901 ledger listed an entry for a young girl, aged 17, named Juliana Roemer. Her father's name was Samuel, and her address matched mine. Cause of death was listed as "cholera."

In those days, the founder of the mortuary would have driven his horse and buggy out to the house, embalmed Juliana in her bed, and most likely would have laid her out in the parlor of the house for one, two, or three days for the wake. After that, she would have been loaded up on a horse-drawn hearse and taken to the cemetery where real gravediggers, not backhoes, dug her hole and bricked out a grave liner.

I ran my finger down the dusty gilded page and located the section and lot in the old city cemetery where Juliana was laid to rest.

These days, my wife and I go out once a year to the old city cemetery and lay flowers on Juliana's grave on the anniversary of her death, and though things really haven't changed at home, I no longer have to hunt for my keys in the morning anymore.

Sara still won't sleep alone with a ghost in the house.

If you would like to submit your story for consideration in future compilations, please send it to Ken and Todd at www.menofmortuaries.com.

Acknowledgments

First and foremost I'd like to thank my agent, Elana Roth. In a literary landscape littered with apathy, she chose this manuscript and championed it, and ultimately made all this happen. Also, my editor at Kensington, Amy Pyle, who helped me produce the best possible finished product. To Bill Thompson, who I have had a relationship with as long as I have been scribbling, thank you for getting the ball rolling. Your advice on the original draft made all this happen.

I'd also like to thank my biggest backers and fans, my grandparents, Jean and Max Robinson. When I embarked on this crazy dream of writing you never doubted me. A special kudo to Barbara and Kruger; my beautiful wife, Melissa, who had to suffer the humiliation of our first date; my uncle, Rick, who taught me *the* trade, and all those I work with (you know who you are). To my peer reviewers: Megan Baker and Caitlin Navarro, I know some material you loved didn't make it into the final product, but your advice on the thousands of drafts was, as usual, point on. And a special thanks to Scott Navarro for the author picture. Finally, my bro, Scott, and all the soldiers like him keeping our country safe.

—Todd Harra

I want to thank my sister, Katie; my grandmothers, Alyce and Katie; and Dr. Bob and Bill W. All these people have given direction and meaning to my life.

As this book was nearing publication, my mother and her mother and my paternal grandmother all passed away unexpectedly and peacefully.

My mother always taught me that you can obtain anything in life that you want. She proved this when she became a commercial pilot in 1978. One of her big life secrets: "Always be able to laugh at yourself."

My grandmothers taught me many things: how to fish, bake, and even knit. And the secret for keeping cookies soft: "Place a piece of bread in your cookie jar, and your cookies will always be moist."

—Kenneth McKenzie

In Loving Memory

16 YEARS
1938

80 YEARS
2002

ALYCE K. MCKENZIE
APRIL 28, 1922–FEBRUARY 15, 2008

People usually ask me where my freewheeling sense of adventure comes from—writing a book like this, for example—and I tell them, hands down, it came from my grandma. My grandma's unique sense of humor and spirited personality shaped my life and helped me achieve all that I have. I think the above photos show her personality. In the photo on the left the year was 1938, my grandma was 16, and she had just been at the Solano County Fair. Alyce—grandma—saw what were billed as "Live Nude Dancers" there (behind wooden fences, of course—it was 1938, after all). Later, tooling around with her friend Dorothy in Alyce's Model T, they came upon a wooden fence. Dorothy posed a dare. Sixty-four years and a lot of bragging later, how could Alyce top that photo? Do it again at age eighty! Grandma, this book is dedicated to you.

—Kenny

A portion of the proceeds from *Mortuary Confidential* is being donated to KAMM Cares Foundation to help women battling breast cancer. For more information or to make a donation, please visit www.kammcares.org.

KAMM CARES
Cancer Foundation

"Coping through comfort."

Founded December 2005

www.KammCares.org